I Am Brahman

SUKHDEV VIRDEE

Copyright © 2019 Sukhdev Virdee

All rights reserved.

ISBN: 9781795634663

DEDICATION

Dedicated to the Absolute Divine
Truth That **YOU** Are!

Whole heartedly dedicated to
Lord Krishna, Lord Shiva,
Sri Ramana Maharshi and
Guru Nanak Dev Ji who have been and are
My Spiritual Guides on the path to
Self Realization and God Realization.

CONTENTS

	Acknowledgments	i
1	Introduction	1
2	Meeting Swamiji	7
3	Aham Brahma Asmi	17
4	The Five Sheaths	31
5	Vatsalya Market Place	53
6	Midnight Talk With Swamiji	65
7	Panshul's Fair	87
8	Panshul's Talk	99
9	Extra Notes	113
10	About The Author	117

ACKNOWLEDGMENTS

There are three friends that I have to absolutely acknowledge who knowingly or unknowingly led me to realize the Absolute Truth.

The first is Vik Sharma, the most hyperactive friend I have. He introduced me to Lord Krishna.

The second friend is Rajeev Aryan, an awakened being himself. He introduced me to the Bhagavad Gita and predicted that I would soon have a similar awakening.
This led to Self-Realization through complete surrender, love and devotion.

The third friend is Ranjan Sahu, a living encyclopedia of Spiritual Scriptures. He was sent by Lord Krishna to guide me on the path of knowledge, the Highest Truth.
This led to God-Realization through direct experiential knowledge.

INTRODUCTION

This is the 2nd part of the series, "I Am Consciousness". In the 1st part titled, *"See God With Open Eyes"* the main character of the series, David, a much sought after heart surgeon in New York City, arrives in New Delhi to embark on a spiritual journey of his life.

He is received by his local guide Uchit and Yogiji from Swamiji's ashram in the Himalayan village known as Vatsalya Village. Three of them travel from New Delhi by train to Dehradun and from there by taxi to the ashram. In the almost eleven hour long journey, Yogiji explains to David what Brahman is and how to experience Brahman in every moment of his life.

He explains the definition as given in the Taittiriya Upanishad. By the time they arrive at the ashram, David has fully understood what Brahman refers to and is able to recognize Brahman everywhere, every time and in everything. Upon arriving at the ashram, while checking in at the reception area, David sees a picture of Swamiji on the wall with a saying beneath it, "Aham Brahma Asmi".

David asks the monk behind the counter what the saying means and the monk replies, *"Sir, Aham Brahma Asmi means I Am Brahman."* David is shocked by the thought that Swamiji thinks himself to be Brahman or God and feels he has come all this way to meet a fraud guru and he is quite eager to meet Swamiji and find out the truth of the claim that Swamiji can show you God.

This 2nd part of the series is a continuation from the 1st and we highly recommend you read the 1st part if you haven't as yet. You would, without a doubt be able to recognize Brahman everywhere, every time and in everything without resorting to blind faith or belief. Brahman has been explained beautifully in the 1st part and in this 2nd part, David is about to realize that his true nature is that very Brahman and that he is One with the Universe, immortal and pure bliss. Happy reading...

I AM BRAHMAN

I
Am
Brahman

I AM BRAHMAN

MEETING SWAMIJI

Yogiji had excused himself earlier as he lived in another part of the ashram. David and Uchit had to share a room. When they reached, the young monk opened the door to a small room that had two single beds with pillows and a heavy folded blanket on each bed. There was a small dressing table and a study table right opposite the beds. On one side of the beds was a door leading to a bathroom that had a simple showerhead, washbasin and western toilet. Neatly placed on the study table was a small booklet with tourist attractions in Vatsalya Village.

"The dining hall is right across the lawn opposite your room. Don't be late, Swamiji is very particular about time," said the young monk pointing to a building with several square shaped windows before closing the door behind him. Both David and Uchit quickly unpacked and took a shower in turns. The water was freezing cold and David just managed just to splash a

little water over his face, hands and feet, shaving his beard and quickly getting dressed. They left the room walking hurriedly along the corridor that led towards the dining hall. The lights were on and there seemed to be more than a few people in the hall.

A smiling monk greeted them at the entrance and pointed them to two long mats that were laid out on the floor. A few people were already seated on the mats facing each other while others who had just walked in joined them. David heaved a sigh of relief at realizing he wasn't the only foreigner at the ashram. There were a few Europeans and Chinese looking people apart from the majority that consisted of Indians.

Everyone sat on the mats cross-legged and one monk was laying out a large banana leaf in front of each person while another handed out two small steel bowls to everyone. A couple of other monks were serving the dinner, which consisted of rice, yellow *dal* (lentils), *chapattis* (freshly baked bread), a mixed vegetable curry and drinking water. From medium sized metal buckets, the rice, *chapatti* and curry was served on the banana leaf while the *dal* and drinking water was poured into the bowls. No one had touched the food and most of the people were frequently looking towards the hall entrance.

Just above the entrance was a large clock that showed about a minute and few seconds before it would strike seven o'clock. Suddenly everyone stood up, even the serving monks stood still and looked towards the entrance as a man with long orange flowing robes stepped into the hall bare foot. Swamiji was quite a tall man, almost six feet two inches, with brown wheatish complexion. His face was glowing, the long beard was pure white and the ends of his moustache were curled upwards. With a smile on his face he walked in greeting everyone with folded hands and nodding his head as he passed by them.

David felt tremendous warmth and love as Swamiji passed him and went to the front between the two rows. There was a small mat laid on which Swamiji sat facing everyone else. To David it resembled a long dining table that seated about twenty-eight to thirty people, the only difference being that this was *on the floor!*

Swamiji was at the head of the table with the two rows of devotees on either side in front of him. The serving monks quickly laid out and served the same food before Swamiji. No one had spoken a word. Swamiji folded his hands, closed his eyes and said something in Sanskrit that sounded like a prayer. David looked around and everyone had their hands folded and eyes closed. David quickly followed suit.

After the prayer, everyone dug into the food. David looked at Uchit to see how the meal was to be had without any cutlery. Uchit had already poured the *dal* from the bowl onto the rice and was mixing it with his fingers. *"That's disgusting!"* thought David but soon decided to give it a shot, *"When in Rome, do as the Romans do. When in India, do as the Indians do,"* he consoled himself.

Imitating what the others did, he broke a piece of the *chapatti*, folded and scooped some vegetable curry into it and lifted it into his mouth, *"Hmmmm, this tastes delicious. It's like a little 'miniature taco' filled with vegetable curry,"* he thought he was doing great until he got to the *dal* and rice. Having poured the *dal* over the rice he began mixing it with his fingers. It really felt weird at first but soon it became fun and he thought, *"I got this! It's easier than it looks!"* But the real fun began when he tried to carry the mixed *dal-rice* with his fingers to his mouth. All the rice seemed to slip out of his fingers. Each time he tried it just a few grains of rice reached his mouth.

He looked at all the others; some were struggling while others did it effortlessly. Uchit looked at David struggling with the *dal-rice* and burst out laughing. The *dal-rice* kept falling from his fingers and the yellow *dal* was now dripping from David's hands down to his elbow.

David picked up the banana leaf and brought it closer to his mouth after which he quite comfortably managed to finish the meal. Almost everyone else including Swamiji had soon finished their meal. Swamiji stood up and said, *"I'll see all of you in the lawn after thirty minutes for an evening walk and some introductions."* After Swamiji had walked out everyone collected their banana leaves and bowls, stood up and headed towards what seemed like a long washing basin. They dropped the banana leaves in a trash can placed at one end of the hall and proceeded to wash the bowls that they had used. Everyone washed their own bowls and put them on a drying rack on the side of the washbasin.

People were now talking to each other. Some had come to the ashram a few days earlier, some were visitors from the village and were going to return home after dinner and a few others, just like David, had arrived that same day.

Everyone seemed friendly, cheerful and happy to be in the ashram. David introduced himself to a few of the other visitors and got to know that people had come from across the globe, he wasn't the only one! There was a couple in their early thirties from Australia, an old man from Germany, a group of four men in their early fifties who were reuniting after college at the ashram. Some Chinese looking couples were actually Indians from the state of Assam, which touches the border of India and China.

Everyone interacted and introduced themselves to each other as they walked towards the garden area where chairs had been laid out in a circle. In the middle was round shaped pond that had different types of fish in it, red lilies floating above the water surface and some dragon flies flew around the flowers. Two bonfires had been lit outside the circle of chairs and it was quite chilly and cold. David was used to cold weather, it does go below freezing point in New York during the winter. Uchit on the other hand was shivering even though he was wearing a fur jacket, cap and woolen scarf around his neck.

Everyone walked on the tiled path around the garden for a few minutes before taking a seat and soon Swamiji came and joined them. *"Welcome everyone, it is my pleasure and honor to have you here with us at the ashram. Some of you have been here a few days already and I'd like to especially welcome those who have joined us today. It would be great if those who arrived today could give a little introduction about yourselves to everyone so when you bump into each other, you don't act like strangers and interact and feel comfortable around each other. I believe we have four new guests today. Can you raise your hand if you arrived today."*

Five people raised their hands, the white couple in their early thirties, the old European man, Uchit and David himself. *"I see five people raised their hands. There must be some mistake but we'll carry on. Okay, who's going to go first?"* asked Swamiji. David looked around and thought he'd go last.

The white couple raised their hand and the man introduced himself and his wife as Oliver and Amelia. They were newlyweds from Melbourne city in Australia. Being childhood sweethearts who went to the same pre-school, high school and college, they were quite comfortable with their live-in relationship but recently decided to tie the knot for the sake of their baby that was on the way. Amelia was two months pregnant and Oliver didn't want the baby to be born to unmarried parents.

Next, the old European man in his late sixties introduced himself as Otto from Germany. He was a widower, his wife had passed away a couple of years back and he was looking for a deeper meaning to life. Having achieved most of what he'd wanted to achieve, he still felt like something was missing. He had been a successful businessman in the import-export business but had now retired and had the time to devote to God and spirituality.

David was next, *"Hi everyone, my name is David and I'm from New York City. I'm a heart surgeon by profession but a very intense spiritual seeker within. I have a burning desire to meet God. I want to meet the Creator of this whole creation and know Him or Her better before I leave this beautiful world. I have no complaints about life, but only gratitude for God and I want to meet him one-on-one to personally thank Him. I don't think that is too much to ask. I'm just in search for someone who can show me God and that search has brought me here."* Everyone was staring at David and he realized he better stop before he utters something that might sound stupid or foolish.

Back home in New York most people didn't have time for such questions and most of his friends only had time for God on the weekends when they went to the local prayer home to remind God that they loved Him and ask for things they wanted in return for their love. But here, to his surprise, he got a nice round of applause for what he had just said. Uchit elbowed David, *"And this is Uchit who has joined me from Delhi. I have hired his services as a personal tour guide during my stay in India."*

Uchit smiled and waved his hand at everyone. *"Aha! That explains the extra fifth person,"* said Swamiji *"The staff must not have been aware of you joining us here. I welcome you all once again."*

"I'm sure it must've been a tiring day for you and I won't keep you for long at all. In fact, for tonight all I want you to do is look at the moon, observe the moonlight that is shining and lighting up the garden and especially note the same moonlight falling in the pond here before you. That is today's homework, now you may take leave to your rooms but if you'd like to have the walk around the garden, please feel free."

"Otto, Oliver, Amelia, David and Uchit, I will see you again in the morning. Goodnight everyone and have a good sleep." "Goodnight Swamiji," replied everyone with folded hands. Having said that Swamiji took leave and walked off towards his room in the ashram.

David and Uchit were tired as well but David decided to walk once around the garden just to observe what Swamiji had asked them to do. It seemed like a normal moonlit night but decided to give Swamiji the benefit of doubt. As some of the devotees left for their rooms, some did decide to take a walk around the garden.

After completing one round during which he intently looked up to observe the moon, looked around the garden that was lit up by the moonlight and finally looked into the pond which also reflected the moonlight and a small shimmering reflection of the moon as well, he decided it's time to hit the sack.

"There doesn't seem to be anything fishy about the man so far. He seems humble and respectful." David thought as they walked back towards their room, *"He sat on the floor and ate the same dinner. In the garden too he sat on one of the simple chairs like the rest of us and spoke with such great love and respect. The staff gave no special treatment to him. But what a waste of time, I could have described the moonlight with my eyes closed if he had asked. There's nothing special about the moon here. The moon shines in the same way all over the world, why would it be any different here?"*

David couldn't wait to have a one-on-one meeting with Swamiji to ask him the personal questions that were now bothering him. He also wanted to test Swamiji to know for sure he was the right Guru and not a fraud. *"I guess we'll find out tomorrow, right now I really need the sleep,"* thought David as they snuggled into their beds and Uchit switched off the light.

AHAM BRAHMA ASMI

Next morning, there was a loud knock on the door. Uchit hesitantly struggled to open his eyes and get out of the warm blanket. *"Good morning, I hope you had a good sleep. Swamiji will meet you at the lawn at 6:30am,"* said a young monk as he handed Uchit a tray with a teapot, some bread toast and butter.

"Sir, wake up, a monk was at the door. He said Swamiji will see us at 5:30am." David looked at his watch, *"Holy cow! We have just half an hour to get ready!"* They both scrambled to get ready, locked the door, ran along the corridor and out onto the lawn where it was still dark, around five chairs had been lined up all facing one main chair. The same monk who had woken them up was clearing the area and the garden.

"Hey, where is Swamiji and everyone else?" asked David. *"Swamiji will be here at exactly 6:30am,"* came the reply, *"What!"* exclaimed David looking at Uchit, *"You said 5:30am!" "I must have not heard correctly sir."* The monk walked up to them and said, *"Sir you're an hour early, it's still 5:30am" "I know, but we're all ready and set now. I guess we'll just wait for Swamiji here,"* said David.

"Sir, the Sun is about to rise in another thirty minutes. If you please I can show you a place from where you can enjoy the early morning Sunrise of the Himalayas. It's at the top of a nearby hill. You won't regret it I promise," said the monk. *"Sure, that would be great,"* said David. *"Sir, I'll just be back. Do you prefer tea or coffee?" "Coffee,"* replied David.

He soon returned with a thermos flask in one hand and some paper cups placed over it. *"Follow me,"* he said. They went out the ashram gate and carried on walking on the road alongside the hill. At one point the monk stopped and pushed aside some bushes, which revealed a kind of footpath that didn't look like it was used frequently. The trail led them to an almost vertically steep hill. As they climbed to the top, panting and out of breath, David looked at the other side of the hill that revealed an unbelievable scenery.

Right off the edge from where they were all standing was a deep vast valley filled with exotic trees, bushes and flowers and butterflies of different colors playing in the cool breeze at the crack of dawn.

Across the horizon they could see where the Sun was beginning to pierce its first rays through the sky. They all sat on the grass and watched as the sun seemed to be writing poetry in different colors with light, slowly bringing to life the entire Earth where its rays touched. The monk poured and handed out the coffee. The three of them sat in silence as in the next few minutes the world seemed to wake up, birds chirped in the trees, flew from one tree to another while others painted perfect v-shaped lines across the sky.

It was like a scene from the movies, only this was real. The cool wind blowing across their faces, the steam rising from their coffee cups, the moist wet grass they were sitting on, the different animals coming out of their hiding places and the stillness of the entire landscape had them all completely awestruck and mesmerized by the magic that was unfolding before them. The Sun was up in all its glory as the golden sunlight proved yet again to be the most precious gold found on Earth. It felt like God was saying, *"Hello?"* Time stood still as the Creator revealed and brought to life His creation in the most beautiful and artistic way.

"Quick, we must hurry back or we'll be late!" exclaimed the monk breaking the silence. *"Oh no! It's almost 6:30am. Let's go!"* screamed David jumping to his feet. After reaching the ashram they ran towards the lawn where they could see Swamiji already seated and sitting opposite him were Otto and the Australian couple, Oliver and Amelia.

"Come come," said Swamiji waving his hand, *"Take a seat. I'm really sorry I forgot to mention our day starts quite early here compared to the city life that you would be accustomed to. Nevertheless, we're all here now. Take a moment to settle down and then we'll begin. Last night you introduced yourselves to the rest of the people staying at the ashram. This morning I want to get to know you personally and find out how better I can serve you. I would like to know what you are seeking and why. Let's start with you Otto,"* said Swamiji.

"Well, like I said last night, I lost my wife two years back and I'm looking for a deeper meaning to life. I've worked hard, earned an honest living, served the community in various ways but I still feel unsatisfied deep within. I'm not getting any younger now and would like to spend the rest of my days dedicated to the Supreme God. Maybe wash away a few of my past sins and look forward to going to heaven."

"That's great," said Swamiji, *"So you're seeking God and would obviously like to go to heaven after you leave the body. That's what most people seek to do after retirement. They would like to do all the things they couldn't do in their younger working years which include serving and worshiping the Lord so as to please Him, gain some peace of mind and become a deserving candidate to go to heaven after death. What I say might sound a little crude and raw but I communicate my honest feelings. It's better that we see things as they truly are and not the way we would like to see them. Oliver and Amelia, what brings you here? You should be somewhere on the beaches of Australia enjoying your honeymoon and celebrating the baby that's on the way."* Swamiji said jokingly.

"Swamiji," Oliver spoke, *"You're right and yes most people in our place would be doing exactly that. But you see, we have been together long enough and we've outgrown the early romantic getaways that newlywed couples crave for. I feel we're mature enough to know that we do love each other a lot and we have been there, done that, as far as the honeymoon period is concerned. I think the best way to put it would be to say that we're here to find out who we truly are and what is the purpose of this life. We want to be in touch with our real nature so that we can live life in the most harmonious way that we can."* Amelia nodded in agreement.

"That's great too. It is important in life to know who you truly are. There isn't any point of doing anything worthwhile in life if you do not know who the 'doer' is in reality. It should be common sense to know oneself before attempting to know anyone or anything else. Yet we are never taught that by anyone, not even in school or by our parents sadly enough," Swamiji looked at David and continued, *"David we heard what you said last night about your desire to meet God and talk to Him. You're looking for someone who can show you God. Would you like to add anything more to that?"* asked Swamiji.

"Yes," replied David, *"I have a few questions for you Swamiji, can I ask them?"* asked David in a rather serious tone of voice. *"Of course you can, please go ahead,"* said Swamiji. *"Swamiji have YOU seen God and can you show me God?"* Swamiji looked and smiled at David, *"My child, God cannot be seen. God is always the Subject. He, She or It can never be the Object of perception. You can never see God because God is always the Seer. You cannot hear, smell, taste, touch, imagine, describe, draw, experience or perceive God in any way because God is always the PerceivER or the ExperiencER, and never the perceived or the experienced."*

"The problem with man today is that he thinks, 'when I meet God, I will be here and there will be God'. That is impossible! God can never be the Object of anyone's perception. So, to answer your question David I haven't seen God because I am 'made' of the same substance as Him. The reality of God and my reality are one and the same. I cannot show you God, I can only point you to your true nature which is absolutely one with God." Swamiji explained in a very polite manner.

"Are you Brahman?" asked David with a little anger in his voice now. Swamiji looked David in the eye and said, *"Aham Brahma Asmi. Yes, I am Brahman."* David could no longer control himself, *"Swamiji, you're claiming that YOU are Brahman! That YOU are the One Absolute Reality of the entire Universe! You mean to say YOU are present everywhere at the same time and in every object in the Universe. The entire Universe is nothing apart from YOU. This chair is you, the grass is you, the birds singing there are you, the clouds, the walls, the trees and everything I see here in reality, is YOU? Is that what you're trying to say? Are YOU God?"* David's hands were shaking now as he asked all this. Otto, Oliver and Amelia were in shock, stunned by what they were hearing.

"Tat Tvam Asi," said Swamiji very calmly, *"David, I must say I am very impressed with you. Yogiji and Guruji (both characters are in part one) are very good at explaining what Brahman is, but you my child, have understood it perfectly. It will be a pleasure and honor imparting my knowledge and sharing my wisdom with you. You have understood Brahman perfectly. Everything you can perceive in anyway is Brahman. There is nothing apart from Brahman in this Universe and the Universe is nothing but Brahman. Now the question you are asking is, if everything is Brahman then who or what are you, me and everyone else?"* Swamiji knew exactly what was going on in David's mind. *"The answer to that is 'Aham Brahmasmi – I am Brahman. If you don't understand that then try to understand 'Tat Tvam Asi' – That Thou Art."*

David looked puzzled but a little calmer now, *"What does that mean?" "It means I am that Absolute Reality and so are YOU and everyone else. If you know yourself as you truly are, you will realize that you ARE already Brahman. This is the birthright of every human being on Earth but only a handful are usually interested in finding out and are willing to do what it takes to realize it. Of those interested one in a million actually does what is required to realize God or the Self. Those are the ones we call the Enlightened Ones, the Saints, the Sages, the Gurus and the Buddha's of the world."*

"They all realized their true reality and became one with God or 'awakened' from the dream called life. They realized their true Brahman nature. After Self Realization or God Realization they then dedicate the rest of their worldly lives to helping others do the same. Their common message is always, "I have realized the Absolute Reality or I have Awakened to the Truth and you can too IF you are willing to do what it takes."

"The true realized Guru, Saint or Sage would never say that "I have realized the Absolute Reality but YOU cannot realize it, or that I have awakened to the Absolute Reality but YOU cannot do the same. Run away from anyone who claims that." Everyone was silent as Swamiji spoke with great authority, yet his voice full of love and compassion."

"Otto, Oliver and Amelia, please don't look puzzled, I have some good news for you too. He who searches for God finds himself and he who searches for himself finds God. The reality of God and your true Self is one and the same. These are simply different paths and you can take whichever path appeals to you BUT the goal and truth arrived at, is always ONE and the same. That is, you and God are one and the same thing in reality. There is no God apart from You and there is no you 'apart' from God. You are one with God and the only thing is that you do not know it."

"However, most people misunderstand these statements, thinking that someone, in his or her limited body and mind is claiming to be God. This is NOT what I am saying nor do the Holy Scriptures say that at any point of time. So, don't think that the person David, sitting here limited to this body and mind is God. No, what you TRULY are, your TRUE nature and the TRUE nature of God is one and the same. Find out the truth of who YOU are or find out the truth of who God is without a doubt, and you'll find that it is one and the same."

"So, before you go out thinking that Swamiji is claiming to be God or Brahman in his little body and mind, I urge you to first keep your mind open to discovering what you came here to seek. In Oliver and Amelia's case you are searching to discover your TRUE nature or who you TRULY ARE and in David's case, searching to discover the TRUE nature of God." Swamiji looked at their astonished faces, which were filled with curiosity that almost screamed, *"Please tell us NOW!"*

David spoke as if breaking off from the trance created by Swamiji's words. *"Swamiji, if it's true that I am Brahman then it's equally true that I don't know it, feel it or experience it. I'm not doubting you but how can this be possible?"* asked David. *"Please repeat what you understood about the definition of Brahman,"* said Swamiji. *"Brahman is Existence, Consciousness and Infinity simultaneously. I understand that and agree with logical reasoning that there is one pure existence and pure consciousness underlying the entire Universe."* Swamiji interrupted sharply *"If everything that exists is Brahman. Do YOU exist?"* asked Swamiji.

"Yes, of course," came David's reply. *"If everything is perceived through consciousness, are YOU conscious?"* Swamiji was being quick. *"Yes Swamiji, I am conscious but how can I be Brahman? If this is the case then it also means that every living creature is Brahman, every person is Brahman. This tree is Brahman, that bird is Brahman; this flower is Brahman and so on. BUT every person is conscious individually and every person exists, so is everyone a Separate Brahman? How many Brahmans are there in the Universe?"* asked David trying hard to phrase his questions with clarity.

I AM BRAHMAN

"There is only One Brahman – One Absolute Reality," came Swamiji's reply. *"Okay then why do I feel separate from everything outside my body? I am an individual, a person who has his own mind and decides what I want to do. This is the same for every living creature; they have their own mind and decide what they want to do. If everything including all living creatures are ONE Brahman, why does every living creature feel separate from the rest of the Universe, why does everyone fear something, why is there a sense of competition among beings, to be more successful than others, why are people selfish, why do we have to struggle just to survive? Surely why would all this happen if we were all ONE SUPREME BEING?"* asked David thinking to himself. *"Wow! Where did all these questions pop into my head from?"*

Swamiji replied with such compassion and love, it would be difficult to concentrate on his words just because of the unconditional love and grace that was oozing in his presence. *"The reason you and most people don't feel this way is because you don't know that you ARE already Brahman. And the reason you don't know that you are Brahman is because of 'ignorance'. When you came here last night and everyone was seated, you looked around, but did you know who Otto was? No, but once Otto was pointed out to you, it was the same situation, with everything still as it was, but now you knew who Otto was. Prior to that you were 'ignorant' of Otto. The only thing that changed was your KNOWLEDGE of who Otto is.*

The knowledge was always there, it was just pointed out to you. In the same way you are ignorant of your true identity and once you gain knowledge about it, you'll realize everything is still exactly how it was BUT now you 'know' your reality. The sky remains to appear blue even after we gain the knowledge that it is colorless, the mirage still looks like water even after we know its reality."

Swamiji continued, *"In the Mundaka Upanishad (3rd Mundaka, Chapter 2 Verse 9), it says;* **"The knower of Brahman becomes Brahman."** *"How is that possible Swamiji?"* David interrupted abruptly, *"If I know this tree I don't become the tree. If I know this chair, I don't become the chair. So how can the Upanishad make such a bold claim?"*

"Absolutely right my dear. You don't 'become' what you know. You can only become something after knowing it in only ONE case. If you were ALREADY that thing and for some reason did not know it."

"You ARE already Brahman, you just don't know it. You are ignorant of your true nature and once you know it through the right knowledge, you will abide as you already truly are, which is Brahman. The Upanishad means to say, when ignorance (of Brahman) is removed by knowledge (of Brahman), the knower (Brahman) abides (stays or remains) as the known (Brahman). You already ARE and have ALWAYS BEEN only Brahman, after realization you will still abide as Brahman BUT now you will know it directly."

Otto, Oliver and Amelia were totally engrossed in the discussion-taking place. David was the only one who had understood Brahman properly prior to his arrival at the ashram. The rest had a vague idea about Brahman but weren't interested in knowing it and so Swamiji hadn't felt it necessary for them to have Yogiji and Guruji explain it to them. He knew David was the right candidate for Yogiji and Guruji to impart their knowledge to. This is why Yogiji went to receive David from the airport and accompanied him to Guruji's place for a talk before coming to the ashram. Otto, Oliver and many others staying at the ashram didn't get this privilege and had arrived on their own.

David continued, *"Okay I understand Brahman is Existence & Consciousness Infinity. I exist, you exist, he exists and everyone in the ashram exists too. The existence may be the same but I am conscious, you are conscious, he is conscious, everyone is 'independently' conscious. Your consciousness is not my consciousness or anyone else's consciousness, it is only yours and the same applies for every living being that's conscious. How do you explain that there is only ONE Brahman?"*

THE FIVE SHEATHS

"Great observation David. You need to find out WHO is asking these questions and WHO really is in ignorance." "What does that mean Swamiji? I am David, I know that I am David. I'm a man, thirty-six years of age and I'm from New York City. I'm a heart surgeon. What more would you like to know about me?" asked David looking confused. *"All the things you just mentioned are ABOUT you, they're not you!" "Okay Swamiji, then I am here sitting before you. That is all I can say,"* replied David.

"That is a good starting point to find out who or what you truly are," said Swamiji. "You have understood Brahman intellectually but not 'experientially.' Like everyone else, you still feel you are 'limited' in space, time and object identity. You cannot be infinite, right?" asked Swamiji.

David replied, *"Of course I am limited in all three and so is everyone else including you Swamiji. Are you everywhere, every time in everything?"* Swamiji nodded in the affirmative. *"Well I don't know about you Swamiji but as far as I am concerned, I am limited in space, my body occupies only a small amount of space, it doesn't occupy the entire Universe. In time too I know for a fact I am limited. I was born and am certain I will die someday. I won't live forever; I'm not eternal or timeless. What is born is sure to die. And regarding Object Identity, of course I am just me and not any other person or object out there. I'm not even just any David, I'm limited to being only this David. So yeah, I'm pretty sure I'm NOT Brahman!"* exclaimed David.

"Almost everyone in the world thinks of themselves in the same manner and you are not any different. There is absolutely nothing wrong with that. We all have different starting points but the end goal is the same. It's good to know who you are because we can start with that knowledge to find out the truth," continued Swamiji. *"You said you are sitting here before me. In reality it is your body that is sitting here on the chair. And you feel that that is you. You are your body. You are 'limited' to this body."* *"Obviously Swamiji, it's the same for everyone,"* David interrupted, *"You may be right but let's take a closer look."*

"Sure Swamiji, if you say so," and Swamiji carried on *"This body is made up of food and is constantly changing my boy. When you were born you had a different body, in your childhood you had a different body, as an adult you have a different body now and in old age your body will surely have changed from what it is now. Was there a DIFFERENT person in all those different bodies?"* asked Swamiji. *"Of course not Swamiji, I am the same person that was in all those bodies. Sure my body changed with time and grew but I am 'inside' it all the time,"* argued David. *"If YOU don't change yet the BODY keeps changing, then how can you be the body? If you were the body, then, when the body changed you should have changed too, but that doesn't happen. You stayed as the same person. So, you and the body must be two separate entities, you and your body. You cannot be the body,"* continued Swamiji. *"Okay. I guess I've never thought of it that way Swamiji. And yes I do see what you mean, the logic and the reasoning is correct."* replied David.

"Good, there are many reasons but let me give you two more as to why you cannot be the body. Oliver, look at your hand. Do you see your hand?" questioned Swamiji. *"Yes certainly."* replied Oliver, *"Do you feel your hand is looking at you?" "No Swamiji, how can it be looking at me?" "Exactly! You are the Seer and your hand is the Seen. You know and experience your hand but you never get the feeling that your hand is looking at or experiencing you! The subject and the object cannot be the same. YOU are always the subject*

and your body is always the object,"

"*Swamiji, what are you trying to prove?*" asked David. "*It's simple my dear, the 'Seer' and the 'Seen' cannot be the same, the 'Knower' and the 'Known' cannot be the same, the 'Experiencer' and the 'Experienced' cannot be the same. The Subject and the Object cannot be the same. This means that since you can 'see' your body, 'know' your body, 'experience' your body then YOU and your body have to be different from each other. Therefore, you CANNOT be your body. What is 'yours' cannot be you, like your clothes, your car, your house, your jacket, your bag, in the same way 'your' body. Do you see why you cannot be the body? It is your body and so it cannot be YOU.*" explained Swamiji ever so lovingly with a constant smile on his face.

"*Hmmmm, interesting, what's the third reason?*" asked David. "*Are you a conscious or sentient being?*" "*Yes of course I'm conscious and sentient.*" "*Are you conscious of your body?*" "*Yes!*" "*Is your body conscious of you?*" "*No!*" replied David. "*What is conscious and what is not conscious cannot be the same thing. That means you and your body aren't the same thing. YOU are aware or conscious of your body but the body cannot be aware or conscious of you! Therefore you cannot be your body.*"

"Swamiji that is very interesting but I still feel like the real me is somewhere inside this body, I can't be anywhere outside this body." Swamiji continued, *"Let's look a little deeper in the body then. The body is alive and this is because of the life forces in the air called 'prana' that you inhale with your breath. These vital life forces make the body come alive and enable your body to function. Your heart beats on its own, your blood runs through your veins on its own, your breathing happens on its own, different enzymes and juices are created in the body all on their own, your food is digested on its own and so on. All these activities happening automatically are enabled by the life forces that you breathe in through your lungs. Could that life force be you?"* asked Swamiji.

"Could be," replied David and continued, *"Without it I would be dead."* *"Really?"* asked Swamiji, *"Lets apply the same three reasons to find out. Firstly, does this life force change? Of course it does, sometimes you are full of energy, sometimes you feel very lethargic, sometimes your heart beats faster than other times, the body falls sick and it recovers and so on. The life force within you keeps changing all the time but do YOU change with it? Is it a different person when you are full of energy and a different person when you are feeling tired? No, it's still the same you. The life forces keep changing but YOU remain the same person. The changing and the unchanging cannot be the same thing, therefore you cannot be the changing life force."*

"Secondly, do you see, know, experience or perceive the life forces? Yes you certainly can. You know when you are energetic; you know when you are sick, and when you are healthy. You know that your heart is beating; you know you are constantly breathing in and out and so on. The life forces are known, experienced and perceived by you. As we said earlier, the Subject and the Object cannot be the same; The Knower cannot be the known. YOU are the knower and the life forces are known. Therefore you cannot be the life force."

"Third reason. YOU are a conscious and sentient entity. Is the life force conscious or sentient? You are conscious of the life forces running through your body, the life forces aren't conscious of you. Your automatic breathing or beating of the heart cannot be aware or conscious of you. YOU are aware of the life forces, they cannot be aware of you. Therefore you cannot be the life force!" said Swamiji.

"This is very interesting Swamiji, then where am I in the body?" asked David rather curiously. *"Let's look deeper my dear. Something that's subtler than your physical body and intangible that you can be is your mind." "Yes, that would be correct Swamiji. I am my mind within this body." "Not so fast my boy, let us apply the same logic and reason it out before jumping to conclusions."*

"To begin with, does the mind change? Yes it does. The mind is made up of thoughts and of course thoughts change all the time. What you were thinking before you got here, your thoughts of last night, this morning and what you're thinking now would mostly be different thoughts. In fact your mind changes very fast, one moment you want to eat something, the next moment you feel like eating a totally different thing. Your mind keeps changing yet YOU remain the same person. The changing and the unchanging cannot be the same. Therefore you cannot be the mind."

"Secondly, do you know, experience or perceive the mind? Yes you do all the time. You know when you're feeling happy, when you're feeling sad. You experience all the emotions that your mind goes through. You perceive all the different options your mind goes through before deciding on something. You know and experience the mind; your mind doesn't experience you. YOU are the knower and the mind is the known. You are the experiencer and the mind is the experienced. Therefore you cannot be the mind."

"And finally, YOU are conscious of your mind, can your mind be conscious of you? No. Your mind is not a conscious or sentient entity. You can be aware of the thoughts in your mind but the thoughts in your mind cannot be aware of you. Therefore you cannot be your mind!" David was flabbergasted to say the least.

"What or where am I within my body?" asked David. *"We can still go deeper and have a look." "We can???" "Yes, usually someone can argue that they are the 'intellect' part of the mind. You see, the mind comprises of four different faculties. These are the mind, the intellect, the memory and the ego (collectively called the mind). The intellect is that part of the mind that understands, knows and confirms all the knowledge that you possess. For example if I asked you to have a look at that animal on the hill and tell me what it is. When you look and think, that's the mind thinking. When you arrive at the decision that it's a horse, it's the intellect confirming that it's a horse. It does so from stored memory of having seen a horse somewhere prior to now and you confirm that is it a horse, lastly the ego gives you the sense of 'I' and you confirm the statement 'I know that is a horse,'"* explained Swamiji.

"Let's find out if you are the intellect applying the same logic and confirm. Firstly, does the intellect change? Yes. You didn't know something earlier but now you do. Something you know today may be forgotten in a few years down the line. Maybe you didn't understand fractions and decimals in school, later you did understand them and now you've forgotten them again. All this confirmation is being done by the intellect and so yes, it does change all the time. The intellect keeps changing, YOU remain the same person. Therefore you cannot be the intellect."

"Secondly, do you know, experience or perceive the intellect? Of course! You're aware of what you know; you are also aware of what you don't know. I know this is a chair, I don't know how far away Mars is. You are aware of the knowledge in your intellect. Remember, the Knower and the Known cannot be the same. The subject and the object cannot be the same; the experiencer and the experienced cannot be the same. YOU are the subject and the intellect is the object. Therefore you cannot be the intellect."

"Lastly, you are a conscious or sentient entity, is your intellect conscious or sentient? YOU are aware of the thoughts in your intellect, the things you know and those that you don't know, but the thoughts in your intellect cannot be aware or conscious of you. Therefore you cannot be the intellect."

"Swamiji, you're driving me crazy. This is an insane way of thinking but yet completely logical. Is there anything else left within this body that I could be?" asked David. *"Ha ha ha!"* laughed Swamiji, *"We can look into something that's even more subtler than the intangible mind."* *"And what is that Swamiji? I feel like I didn't really learn anything about the human body in medical school,"* said David. *"You see, the physical body which is tangible and that you can touch has another 'subtle body' within it called the mind, which is intangible and you cannot physically see or touch. Now what if we looked beyond the mind?"* *"Beyond the mind? What can there be beyond the mind?"* asked David.

"You see when you are awake, like right now, both your body and mind are active and being used to perceive the world." "Yes, that's right," said David. *"Now when you go to sleep at night, your physical body becomes inactive and you lose awareness of your body. Then you dream and you have a dream body to experience a dream world. You know very well that dreams are created by the mind, which means that even though the body is inactive and not in your awareness, the mind is still active."*

"During the night you also have deep sleep, this is when you don't experience any dreams in sleep. At this time both your body and mind are inactive and you experience the blankness of deep sleep. This is neither the physical body nor the subtle body; it's called the 'causal body'. The Scriptures have names for these different bodies. The physical body is known as the Gross body (Sthula sarira), the life force, the mind and intellect are collectively known as the Subtle body (Sukshma sarira) and the blankness of deep sleep is called the Causal body (Karana sarira). Now let's check whether you are the causal body of deep sleep by applying the same logic we did with the subtle and physical bodies."

"Firstly, does the deep sleep change? Be careful with this one," said Swamiji *"Let me think. Swamiji there's nothing experienced during deep sleep, it's totally blank and stays that way so, no, it doesn't change." "That's absolutely correct!"* said Swamiji sounding very happy. *"The deep sleep state is unchanging. Also your deep sleep state and mine and every other persons deep sleep state are exactly the same. There's no change from one person's deep sleep to another's. Both experience blankness and nothingness in deep sleep."*

"Secondly, do you know, experience or perceive deep sleep?" David scratched his head. *"Of course you do,"* continued Swamiji with vigor. *"Follow this carefully. You experience no-thing in deep sleep. It's not an absence of experience, it's an experience of absence. Nevertheless, you do experience the nothingness. That's why when you wake up you can say or report that you slept like a log, you don't recall anything, you didn't know where you were etc. You report the experience of absence or nothingness or blankness. Remember, the experiencer and the experienced cannot be the same; the knower and the known cannot be the same. YOU are the experiencer and the blankness of deep sleep is the experienced. Therefore you cannot be the causal body."*

"Third reason, are you conscious or aware of deep sleep? While in deep sleep you cannot be aware you are in deep sleep (because of the absence of objects) but the fact that you experienced deep sleep is reported by the mind when you wake up, otherwise you couldn't confirm upon waking up that you slept soundly in deep sleep. Your mind reports that you were conscious or aware of the nothingness or blankness. There was a time in your sleep when no-thing or no object was experienced. After waking up you become aware or conscious of the fact that you experienced deep sleep. Your consciousness and what it is conscious of, have to be different entities, they cannot be the same. Experiencer and experienced cannot be the same. YOU are aware of your deep sleep causal body, it cannot be aware of you. Therefore you cannot be the causal body of deep sleep." Swamiji looked to see if everyone else apart from David was following his words. Otto, Oliver and Amelia simply nodded their heads while Uchit was staring at Swamiji with his mouth open.

David spoke, *"I'm listening Swamiji, please go on, this is going a little beyond the normal way of looking at things." "I agree David, but notice that I didn't say anything that you don't experience on a daily basis. Every single day you experience your physical body, the life force and energy running through your body, your mind thinking, your intellect verifying what you perceive and at night you experience some undisturbed dreamless deep sleep. You go through this every day. I have just made you take a deeper look at all these activities we all take for granted and easily come to the conclusion that we are mortal beings that are limited to this body and mind."* said Swamiji. *"So if my true real Self is not any of these three bodies then who, what or where am I?"* asked David.

Swamiji smiled but didn't say a word. There was total silence for almost a full minute. David was baffled, *"Well? Swamiji, does this mean that I am not in my body, there is no REAL Self or that I don't exist?"* Swamiji looked David in the eye directly and spoke with a hypnotic voice, *"Hopefully you have followed what I said, and realized that you are none of the different aspects of the physical body, the subtle body (mind) and the causal body (deep sleep blankness)."*

"You are not the body. You are not the life force. You are not the mind. You are not the intellect. You are not even the blankness of deep sleep. You are none of those, BUT, are you still here?" "Yes I am here," replied David. *"As WHAT are you still here?"* asked Swamiji. *"I'm not sure,"* spoke Amelia who was following intently with eyes closed, *"I just am. I can't say what it is but it just IS,"* replied Amelia *"You don't know what it is but can you deny that it IS?"* asked Swamiji looking at everyone now. *"No, it just IS,"* replied Amelia.

"As you dropped the other aspects of the body, mind and intellect, mentally try to drop this 'issness' as well," continued Swamiji. *"It can't be dropped,"* said Otto who was also deeply engrossed by now. *"'Is' refers to existence. Are you 'aware' of this issness?"* asked Swamiji, speaking slowly now. *"Yes,"* said everyone except David.

Swamiji carried on, *"You are here and now as pure existence and pure consciousness. Pure consciousness is experiencing its own pure existence. Brahman is aware of itself or is Self-aware. Take a look and see if this "issness" has any kind of size, shape or form, does it have a beginning or an ending?" "No, it has no shape. It has no form. It has neither a beginning nor an ending. It is nothing, but it IS."* Oliver joined into the answers. *"How far is it away from you? Is there any distance between you and this issness?" "No. No distance at all,"* replied Oliver.

"If there is no distance between the issness and you, and I said this 'issness' is you, would that be true? Look carefully before you reply," asked Swamiji. *"Yes it IS me,"* replied Amelia. *"Yes, it is me,"* echoed Oliver, Otto and Uchit. *"THIS is what you are! This is your true reality. This is what you truly are. Is everyone having the same experience right now?"* asked Swamiji. *"Yes,"* replied everyone except David.

"David, what are you experiencing?" asked Swamiji as he'd noticed David had stopped answering his questions. *"I can't see or find this true self or true reality. I don't see this issness that you're talking about too."* David confessed while still maintaining eye contact. Swamiji was very serious now as he spoke, taking a short intense pause after each sentence; he spoke very slowly.

"The One Looking, Is The One You're Looking For. The One Looking, Is Looking For Another Object OUTSIDE Of It To Call Its REAL Self. You Already ARE What You Are Seeking. You CANNOT Be Outside You. You CANNOT Look At You. You CANNOT Perceive You. You Can Only Become Aware Of You. YOU CAN ONLY... BE.... YOU!"

It was like the world had come to a standstill, as everyone was totally mesmerized by Swamiji's words. No one moved for what seemed like eternity. After a few seconds David smiled at Swamiji, *"Why are you smiling David?"* asked Swamiji who was reading David's eyes and face like a book. David smiled again but didn't say a word this time. There was total silence again.

Swamiji pointed a finger at David, *"You Got It!" "You, Have Just Found You! And To Think Of All The Places You Looked For Him. He Was Right Here All The Time. He Was Right Where You Were Looking From. Stop Looking And Simply Be Aware Of The Self,"* David broke out into an uncontrollable laughter. It looked like he was experiencing real joy for the first time. He laughed and laughed while everyone slowly gave into the contagious laughter, soon everyone was laughing in ecstasy. Swamiji looked on smiling quietly, his aura emitting bundles of unconditional love and grace. What a moment they were all experiencing.

He let everyone sink into the ecstasy that they were experiencing for the first time. He knew the joy of this profound self-discovery. Whenever he saw someone experience it for the first time it always brought back memories of when his Guru had made him experience it for the first time. It was a *'taste', a glimpse, a small spray of the ocean of actual real freedom.* Nevertheless, even the smallest glimpse is life changing for the one who has never thought of himself as other than the body with a mind.

"That's great everyone, let's inquire a little more and answer a few more questions whose answers may astonish you. This issness, which you truly are, can it ever be in pain?" "No," came a unanimous reply. *"Can it ever die?"* "No." *"When was it born?"* "It was never born," said Amelia. *"Has it just appeared now after we started*

looking?" "No. It has always been there," replied David. *"Can it ever go away, say like after you sleep and wake up tomorrow morning?"* "No. It can't go away," replied Uchit who was rather enjoying this new discovery now. *"Is there any suffering here?"* "No," *"Can anything destroy it ever?"* "No, it can't be destroyed," replied Oliver. *"Does it want to be rich and famous?"* "No," said everyone while Amelia laughed at the question.

"Let's probe a little further. David, is there anything in the Universe that is different or apart from this?" "No, it is nothing and everything at the same time. There is nothing apart from it," replied David. *"Otto, is there any place in the Universe where this is not?"* "No. It is everywhere," replied Otto carrying on, *"Not only is it everywhere in the Universe, it IS the Universe!"* said Otto sounding excited. *"And this IT or issness is your true reality?"* asked Swamiji. *"Yes. I am the Universe. I am nothing and everything at the same time. Everything is in me."* replied Otto. *"David, would every person have their own such issness 'separate' from this one?"* "No," replied David, *"There is only one issness which is every-one and every-thing. There is nothing in the Universe but this. The Universe is nothing but this. And this is my true reality."* said David rather surprised at what he was claiming.

"David, do you mean that the person sitting here is the Universe?" probed Swamiji. *"No. That is my body with a mind but in reality I am none of those. I am a witness to them and remain untouched by them. My true nature is this issness, and this issness, is the entire Universe. My body and mind are being witnessed by this issness. And if I look from this true nature of mine now, what goes on with my body and mind cannot affect me, the issness, in any way ever,"* said David.

"David, is there any difference between what you understood as Brahman on your way to the ashram and this issness?" asked Swamiji. *"No Swamiji, you can call it Brahman or Issness, it doesn't matter because it just IS,"* replied David.

"Okay, we'll stick with the word from the Upanishads and refer to it as Brahman." Swamiji continued, *"This issness is Brahman. Your true reality is Brahman. Everyone and everything is Brahman. The Universe is Brahman, Brahman is the Universe. There is no second thing apart from Brahman and this Brahman is YOUR true nature. Uchit, does this sound correct?"* asked Swamiji. *"Yes Swamiji. Absolutely!"* replied Uchit smiling. *"This cannot be easily comprehended by the human mind,"* said Swamiji, *"Yet this is the absolute reality."*

"It is the substratum, the one single substance of which the entire Universe is made and YOU Are That! Tat Tvam Asi – That Thou Art!" Exclaimed Swamiji with complete authority. *"Open your eyes Amelia. Brahman is everywhere and you need to realize it with open eyes, not closed. The sky in reality is colorless, yet when you look up it appears to be blue in color, right? In the same way the underlying reality of the Universe is Brahman (Existence, Consciousness, Infinity) - the issness; yet whenever you look around, you see thousands of different types and forms of objects. The appearance doesn't change the reality nor does it even come in contact with the reality ever, it just 'appears' that way. All the water in the mirage cannot wet a single grain of sand."* Swamiji was bursting forth with words of wisdom.

"Are we all enlightened now Swamiji?" asked Uchit with folded hands. *"Ha Ha Ha Ha!"* laughed Swamiji and he kept laughing in the most adorable way for a few seconds. He was like a child who had heard a funny joke for the first time and was replaying it in his head over and over again. Finally getting a hold on himself, *"No my son, it doesn't work this way. You have to 'become' Brahman in the true sense which takes a little time depending on how sincerely one seeks it."*

"But Swamiji you said that the knower of Brahman becomes Brahman. I have known Brahman now, why haven't I become Brahman? You also said I have always been Brahman and now you're saying I still have to 'become' Brahman? You're contradicting yourself Swamiji," said David. *"Let me put it in perhaps another more clearer way,"* said Swamiji.

"The knower of Brahman becomes Brahman is correct. You already are and have always been nothing but Brahman is also correct. Now, when I said you have to 'become' Brahman I meant, YOU have to come into being Brahman.

Brahman is the only reality there is BUT right now there's a false YOU appearing in all of you. When you come into being Brahman, the YOU will merge and disappear into Brahman and all that will be left, was and will always be, Brahman. The false identity will vanish into the true reality. This dissolution of YOU into Brahman takes time and I'll show you in the next few days what you need to do to hasten the process. Only the sincere seeker goes through it, most shy away from pursuing it."

"Not everyone who comes to the ashram of any Guru or Saint becomes enlightened even after staying with them a few weeks or months, while the rare one will become enlightened by just coming into contact with the aura of a true Sage, without uttering a word. So, you've experienced a small glimpse of the Supreme Being who is always there. You know Brahman intellectually and after today you won't doubt its existence. Now it needs to become a living reality for you, which we will discuss in the next few days. This is enough for today, try to soak in what we shared today and I'll just find out if lunch is ready. I don't know about you lot but I'm starving."

"Lunch is ready," announced a monk who was standing right behind Swamiji, no one had noticed him walk in. Everyone was so engrossed in Swamiji's talk. *"When did you come here Ramlal?"* asked Swamiji, *"Swamiji, I walked in quietly and have been behind you for the past ten minutes. I didn't want to disturb your talk as everyone was heavily engrossed, so I waited for the right moment."* *"Very good Ramlal,"* said Swamiji, *"After lunch and a short nap will you be kind enough to take everyone here to the market place?"* *"Of course Swamiji, it will be my pleasure,"* replied Ramlal, the same young monk who had woken up Uchit and David in the morning and taken them to experience the beautiful sunrise of the Himalayas.

I AM BRAHMAN

VATSALYA MARKET PLACE

Ramlal led everyone into the local market area that was a short twenty-minute walking distance from the ashram. As they approached the market area, Ramlal first took them to the local forex bureau to exchange their foreign currency to Indian Rupees. Once everyone was done, they all headed into the market shops independently. Ramlal, showed them all a small fenced circle that had a tall tree in the center and said, *"Please listen up, you all may go into different shops on your own. We will meet up at this spot in exactly two hours from now. It's 3pm, so be here by 5pm. The top of this tree is visible from any part of the market and you can easily find your way back, its known as the 'Witness Circle,' and anyone in the market would direct you here in case you get lost."*

David and Uchit were on their way into the market with Uchit leading the way. Oliver and Amelia took off towards some shops with handicrafts. Otto headed towards some clothes shops. The entire market consisted of only four streets along four blocks of buildings. Most vendors had items placed outside the shops right on the pavements. There were all sorts of activities going on. Food was being cooked on the streets, there were clothes hung on racks, there was a temple where people were praying amidst all the background noise.

There were cows being fed on the roadside, bicycles and cycle *rickshaws* seemed to be the common means of transport. David asked Uchit to look for anything that would be interesting for him to take back home to New York City. Uchit quickly spotted a shop that displayed marble statues and they headed there.

As they entered the shop there were large sculptures of different objects like dolphins, hawks, eagles, flowers, people in action, all made of marble stone. Inside the shop on either side were glass cabinets in which smaller statues of many of the Indian gods and goddesses such as *Ganesha, Shiva, Hanuman, Krishna, Laxmi and Durga* were displayed. Animals such as elephants, camels, and cows all beautifully sculptured in shiny white marble.

David loved a small face of Gandhi sculptured in shiny white marble. He picked it up and examined the details carved into the sculpture. Gandhi's glasses, his smile, every hair of his moustache and his baldhead were perfectly sculptured. *"This is beautiful, how much for this one?"* asked David to the shopkeeper who was dusting some old looking statues. *"Oh, that's for two thousand five hundred rupees sir,"* came the reply. *"That's too much, we'll pay you one thousand five hundred and not a rupee more,"* said Uchit, trying to negotiate on behalf of David.

"I won't accept a rupee less than two thousand, take it or leave it," said the shopkeeper. *"We'll take it, please pack it in such a way that it's safe to carry on a flight,"* said David. *"Sure sir, are you staying at the ashram?"* he asked, *"Yes,"* said David.

Just then a middle aged man with old tattered clothes and white powder all over his hands and clothes walked into the shop from the back door, *"Hey, I need some help, I've got a big one and can't bring it in alone,"* he shouted out to the shopkeeper. *"Okay, just hold on a minute,"* he shouted back. *"Sir, I'll be right back, meanwhile please take a look if you'd like anything else,"* he said and dashed out the back door. Soon both men were struggling to carefully carry in a huge statue of Lord Krishna. They carefully placed it on a marble stand inside the shop. It was around four feet tall, all in white and looked immaculate.

Lord Krishna in his famous pose playing the flute. The crown on his head, his clothes, his crossed feet, his smile and the flute were all so well detailed in marble, David was amazed. *"Who is making these fine sculptures here in Vatsalya? Does anyone buy them here? They are simply fabulous and the workmanship is flawless,"* said David to the shopkeeper, *"Oh yes sir, a few of these are bought by foreigners who visit Swamijis ashram just like yourself and we also supply other shops in the bigger cities like Bangalore, Calcutta, Mumbai and New Delhi. This is Aabha, he is the one who makes these beautiful sculptures at the back of our shop,"* said the shopkeeper.

"Hi, would you like to take a look at our workshop in the backyard?" asked Aabha, *"Of course, it would be a pleasure,"* replied David. Aabha led them through the back door into a back yard where many unfinished sculptures stood. On one side there were big boulders of marble in the shape of big rocks. *"What are you going to do with those?"* asked David pointing at the big rocks. *"Oh those? I'm going to set them free them from their misery in a few weeks,"* replied Aabha.

"What? What kind of misery?" asked David. *"You see this one? This big fat almost round one? It has a mother elephant hidden inside it. I can see her standing with her head and tusks facing up. Her tail is in the air and her front left foot is ahead of the right one. Her mouth is open and her ears too are wide open. She's a beauty isn't she?"* asked Aabha looking at David and

Uchits rather surprised faces.

"Oh you don't see her yet, but I can see all her details already. She is so beautiful, I can't wait to set her free." *"What do you mean by setting her free?"* asked David. *"Oh you don't know? I'm the sculptor and I can see the sculptures in the rocks even before I work on them. The sculptures already exist in the rocks, all I need to do is chip away the unwanted stone and they're set free. See, in that one there's a beautiful dolphin coming out of the water, in the rock besides that one there are two galloping horses. They are already inside the rock, I need not add anything to them but simply chip out what is not them and they'll be revealed in all their glory. It's kind of what Swamiji does as well. You must be here to meet Swamiji, am I right? Of course I'm right!"* said Aabha without giving David a chance to reply.

"It's simple, has Swamiji told you about Brahman?" asked Aabha, *"Yes,"* replied David, *"That's great, because I do exactly what Swamiji does."* *"What? What do you mean by that?"* asked David. *"If you know about Brahman, then you would also be knowing that you are already Brahman?"* *"Yes, so?"* asked David. *"Well Swamiji can't do anything to 'make' you Brahman, all he can and will do is to chip away everything that isn't Brahman and then you'll be left as you truly are. I do exactly the same thing with all these pieces of rocks. Swamiji is the sculptor of your real being, your true reality. Don't resist any part being chipped away by him because everything that he will remove will be something that you falsely*

believe is you," said Aabha.

"He is a true Guru and I have been associated with him for many years. He guided me to realize my true real Self and now I'm completely free of the person I thought I was. You as the person don't get freedom, you get freedom FROM the person you thought you were. Let Swamiji chip and break away all the false notions of who you think you are and you'll shine in all your glory of the real Self," said Aabha.*"You mean you have realized your true nature of Brahman and are living it experientially? And if you have then why are you still working as a sculptor when you can become a Guru and impart this knowledge to others?"* asked David,

"Well, yes I can say with confidence that I have realized the Self and have transcended everything that the world can give or throw at this body and mind. I continue to do the work I love, one need not become a monk because he or she is seeking or has realized his or her true nature. Your inner Self can be a monk without anything showing outwardly," replied Aabha.

"My God, are there other people in the village who are also Self realized?" "Oh yes, quite a few. In fact there are some in the market as well. You must visit 'Panshul's Fair' for a fun way to realize God or the Self. It's open only on weekends and you'll be better off coming in the morning and spending an entire day there. It's located at the northern end of the market," said Aabha.

Inside the shop, the shopkeeper had already packed Gandhi's statue carefully and called out, *"Sir I've packed it carefully so it won't break. Is there anything else that caught your eye? I can discount the prices a little further if you like."* David and Uchit went in, looked around for a little more time and picked up a few smaller display statues of Indian artifacts that he could take back as gifts for his friends back home. They promptly paid the shopkeeper and left with Uchit carrying the shopping bags.

Both walked along one street where clothes were displayed on both sides and they bumped into Oliver and Amelia who were carrying almost ten shopping bags and looking like they were having fun. *"Everything is so cheap here,"* said Amelia, *"I've bought some very good quality clothes and handbags. These same items would cost almost ten times the price back home,"* Amelia continued. David simply nodded his head in agreement. He decided to stick around with Oliver and Amelia as he lost all interest in shopping anything else after the talk with Aabha.

"What a village," he thought to himself, *"Enlightened people doing ordinary jobs and no one can tell they're enlightened. There was no sense of ego or pride at all in Aabha, he was so down to earth and looked happy and content with the work that he was doing, truly worthy of appreciation,"* thought David.

They walked around the shops for some more time with David and Uchit following Oliver and Amelia blindly as David announced he's shopped enough for the day. Uchit suggested that since they weren't shopping any more it would be advisable that they go and wait at the *Witness Circle* for everyone else and David obliged. David and Uchit found their way back to the *Witness Circle* where Ramlal was sitting alone on a nearby bench. They made their way towards Ramlal who immediately got up upon seeing them.

"Sir, did you buy anything?" and Uchit showed him the bags he was carrying. *"Great, we still have sometime before the others come back, would you like to have some mouthwatering golgappe?"* *"Okay, if you say so,"* said David. They walked a few steps towards a small nearby shop where a middle-aged man standing behind a counter was making and serving a variety of delicious looking snacks. *"Raju three plates of golgappe,"* said Ramlal to the person serving.

As the man served them the *golgappe* one by one, David could see the top of the tree in the Witness Circle. He looked up and saw a bird right at the top that looked like a partridge. As he looked around the branches of the tree he saw many more such partridges that were busy jumping from one branch to another, others had nests in the tree that they came in and out of every now and then. They seemed so busy. As David ate the *golgappe* his attention went back to the partridge that was right at the top, after staring at it for a few seconds, he realized that the partridge didn't seem to move at all. It stood completely still. David questioned Ramlal about it, *"That is a Snow Partridge that is found in the higher altitudes of the Himalayas." "Why is this place called the Witness Circle?"* asked David.

"This circle was created by Swamiji and named Witness Circle as a remembrance of what his Guruji used to tell him all the time. "Abide as the witness, not the witnessed," his Guruji always said. *"If you look closely at the tree, right at the top is a snow partridge that does not move at all. It's a statue replica of the real bird. It looks at all the snow partridges on the branches that are busy doing all their different activities. The one at the top is merely a witness to the other birds on the branches. It watches without getting involved in any way. It's what Swamiji refers to as the 'Witness Consciousness' in his talks every now and then."*

"The bird at the bottom occasionally looks up and sees the witness bird but soon gets back to what it is doing. Swamiji's Guruji always said the partridge at the top is you, the real Self, your true nature, which is unaffected by what the bird at the bottom is doing. When you realize that and start living life from that perspective, then all the pain and suffering of the worldly life doesn't affect you at all, you simply witness it all, untouched."

"The partridge at the bottom is like the mind and body, always thinking and doing something. As a result the mind and body goes through all the ups and down in this life and if you identify yourself with this bird (the body and mind), then you will keep saying YOU are happy or sad depending on what the mind and body are going through. All this time the real YOU is silently watching and witnessing everything going on, completely untouched and unaffected. Swamiji created this circle and it is protected by the ashram for the purpose of spreading his Guruji's message through an actual example," said Ramlal.

"Otto, Oliver and Amelia soon arrived at the spot and they all made their way back to the ashram. Upon reaching the ashram, Ramlal served them afternoon tea and announced that Swamiji would meet them at midnight in the garden area for an important talk. *"Please take rest, have dinner and take a nap before coming at midnight as the night could be a long one out here with Swamiji,"* announced Ramlal before disappearing into the kitchen. Everyone made their way towards their rooms as well.

I AM BRAHMAN

MIDNIGHT TALK WITH SWAMIJI

By quarter to twelve midnight, everyone had gathered in the garden area. Ramlal was dusting off the chairs, it was very cold and the wind didn't make it any better. On the flip side, it was a beautiful full moon night. The sky was completely clear and the moon shone brightly, even the stars twinkled brighter than everyone was used to back home. Swamiji came out of his room and into the garden greeting everyone with a smile and folded hands. *"Did you enjoy yourselves at the market?"* he asked everyone. *"It's a small village so, very few shops are available and most people sell the basic necessities or make things that are then sent to bigger cities. I hope Ramlal took good care of you."* Swamiji continued.

"Tonight is the perfect for what we're going to be talking about. As you can see it's a full moon night and there are no clouds at all. The

moon is shining brightly like a huge bulb in the sky, lighting up this entire garden as well," he then turned towards Ramlal, *"Ramlal, please prepare some tea, coffee and snacks for later. Its quite cold already and will become even colder later on."*

Ramlal nodded his head and set off towards the kitchen. *"Yesterday I asked you all to observe the moon, the moonlight shining in the garden and the reflection of the moonlight in the pond before us as well. How many of you managed to do that?"* asked Swamiji. Everyone's hands went up.

"Great, Oliver, what did you notice about the moon?" asked Swamiji, *"Swamiji, the moon looked almost the same as it is right now. There didn't seem to be anything absurd or different in the moonlight here compared to what we see back in Australia every night,"* replied Oliver.

"Is that what everyone observed?" asked Swamiji looking at the rest. *"Yes Swamiji,"* came a chorused reply. *"Well I did ask you to observe, not necessarily compare with other nights or places. The moon is one and the same everywhere. What I wanted you to do is observe and notice things that we usually don't take the time to notice, and as a result we take for granted,"* said Swamiji looking at everyone. Everyone was already feeling bathed in unconditional love and grace as he spoke politely with so much love.

"David, today's talk will answer your question about why each person feels conscious separately if there is only One Existence and One Consciousness called Brahman. Let's take a look at the moon and moonlight together. If you notice carefully the entire garden is lit up by the moonlight. We can see each other and everything around us because of the moonlight reflecting on the objects. However, if you look closely to the reflection of the moon in the pond you will see that there is a small image of the moon being reflected on the water surface. All the other objects around us are reflecting the moonlight but only the water in the pond is reflecting a small image of the source of light along with the light. There are objects that only reflect the light while a few others reflect a small image of the source along with the light."

"Now, if we look into the sky, you'll see the moon shining in a perfect circle because it's a full moon night tonight. The moon however is not a self-luminous object; it is merely reflecting the Sunlight that's falling on it. The entire dark space around the moon is also filled with sunlight but we can't see it because there is nothing for the sunlight to fall on. Sunlight cannot be seen directly by the eyes; in fact any light we see is light that is reflected off the surface of an object. Light cannot be seen directly, therefore we don't see the light around the moon but we do see the light that the moon reflects and call it the moonlight."

"Hypothetically speaking now, if we take the moon to be a person, then the Moon also cannot see any sunlight in space. It can only see other planets, moons and meteors that are reflecting the same sunlight falling on them. If the moon starts to think that it is Self-luminous and gives out light on its own just like the other planets and meteors in space then it would be making a grave error."

"Also thinking that the moonlight is different from the light reflected off different planets is another grave error. The true reality is the Sunlight that enables all the planets and the moon to 'appear' to be shining on their own. The Sunlight is the One True Reality while all moons and planets merely reflect the Sunlight and thus 'appear' to be luminous."

"None of them can see the Sunlight directly to know the source of their light and so they only see other luminous objects shining like themselves in space. This leads to the error of each one thinking that they are Self luminous and shining separately from one another. Thus every shining entity in space appears separate and individual. Are you following me so far? Any questions till this point?" asked Swamiji.

Everyone looked on, no one raised their hands. *"That's okay, if at any point you have a question feel free to stop and ask me,"* said Swamiji before carrying on. *"All the objects in the Universe can broadly be classified into two kinds, those that are insentient and those that are sentient, basically living things and non-living things. The living things all have the life forces (prana) in them and are conscious, aware or have the ability to perceive and respond in some way or another. Living things can be categorized into either the Animal kingdom or the Plant kingdom. Everything else apart from the animal kingdom and plant kingdom falls in the non-living things category.*

Otto raised his hand, *"Swamiji, both living and non-living things are Brahman but non-living things are not conscious so how are they Brahman?"* *"Great question Otto and I was just coming to that. ALL objects in the Universe reflect existence from Brahman and thus they exist, these are all the inert or insentient things. They exist because they reflect ONLY existence from Brahman. Then there are other objects that have subtle bodies (the mind) which have the capacity to reflect BOTH existence and consciousness from Brahman, these are all the conscious or living things."*

"Every living thing has a mind (subtle body) of its own, it is conscious and can perceive the world around it. Thus the living thing not only reflects existence but also consciousness. The mind cannot see Pure Consciousness but it sees other entities like itself that appear to be conscious and concludes that it is separately conscious from other conscious entities. All this while, in reality, all objects are simply reflecting Existence and Consciousness from the One Supreme Being – Brahman."

"Just like the wall here is reflecting ONLY the light of the moon so we can see it, but the water reflects BOTH the light and also a small image of the moon and thus it 'appears' like the moon is shining in the water. The different reflecting surfaces make the difference. Every living thing has a subtle body, which reflects both existence and consciousness from Brahman, while every non-living thing (without a subtle body) reflects only the existence of Brahman and appears to be insentient. So, David, the reality is that there is only One Brahman, which means One Existence and One Consciousness, and due to many subtle bodies it appears to be divided into many. You are conscious in the same way that Oliver or Amelia are conscious, but to recognize and realize from personal experience that it is actually the same ONE Pure consciousness pervading everything is called spiritual enlightenment," said Swamiji with confidence and a childlike sparkle in his eyes.

Everyone remained silent trying to absorb the profound wisdom that Swamiji had just spoken with so much love, compassion and authority. *"David, did you understand that? Is your doubt now cleared?"* asked Swamiji. *"Yes Swamiji,"* replied David. *"Then I'm sure you wouldn't mind summing up this discussion for all of us here,"* said Swamiji putting David on the spot. *"Sure Swamiji, I'll put it across in the best possible way as I can."*

David began, *"There is only One Supreme Being called Brahman which is defined as Pure Existence, Pure Consciousness, Infinity. Everything in the Universe is only Brahman in reality. All objects reflect or borrow existence from Brahman and hence they exist. Some objects (subtle bodies) not only reflect their existence but also reflect consciousness from Brahman and hence they not only exist but also 'appear' to be conscious individually or separately. In reality the physical body is insentient, the life forces (prana) are insentient, the mind and intellect (subtle body) are both insentient but because the subtle body can reflect or borrow consciousness too the mind "appears" to be sentient or conscious and thus the mind concludes that, 'I am a conscious mind with a body,'"* said David.

Everyone was dumbfounded; Uchit clapped as though he had understood every bit of it but if asked to repeat a word of what he heard he wouldn't be able to. Otto, Oliver and Amelia kept looking at David in disbelief of how David had explained everything with such ease and clarity.

Swamiji looked at David and smiled before asking, *"What's the problem David?"* *"Swamiji, I've been a science student and was quite a bright student in school so I really didn't have much difficulty in understanding all this. If everything that I just said is true then it has been of no help at all. What is the point of realizing that I am Brahman? I'm perfectly fine living as an individual with ups and down in my life than realizing that I am everything and become boring. Wouldn't life become very dull with no excitement left anymore?"*

David continued, *"I understood what Brahman is before I came to the ashram thanks to Yogiji and Guruji. Through your grace I now understand that I AM Brahman. I also appreciate that this is all intellectual and philosophical understanding and not experiential as it should be. But what difference will it make once I realize it experientially and start living my life that way? What is on the other side of actual realization of Brahman or spiritual enlightenment that I cannot see from this side?"* asked David.

"I am so pleasantly surprised and happy with what you have just explained about your understanding so far. You truly must've been an A-Grade student in school. Most importantly, your questions are so well put and clear and deserve to be answered because you have shown yourself to be worthy of knowing the answers. One in a million truly care to understand this wisdom and knowledge. One in a million TRULY wants to know God."

"If you ever find someone saying I want to meet God try this little test. Pull out a knife and hold it to their throat and tell them, 'I guarantee that you will meet God, but you have to die first. God is waiting for you in Heaven and the first step towards Him is to die. Are you willing to die right now to go and meet God?'" Everyone burst out laughing.

Swamiji continued, *"Everyone wants to go to Heaven but no one wants to die. Everyone wants to meet God but not at the expense of their life which they consider so precious. Everyone wants the entire Universe but not at the expense of losing what they have. Hardly anyone REALLY wants to meet God or even know God. David, you are an exception and I cannot but help answer all your questions and clear your doubts as you are truly a searcher."* *"A searcher? Don't you mean a seeker?"* asked David.

"When you don't know where to find something, you are seeking it. Once you know where to find something you are no longer seeking but searching for it," replied Swamiji with a smile. *"Let me tell you, hundreds of seekers come to this ashram every year but the 'searchers' I can count on my fingers on one hand. Every one of you, including me here, are blessed by His grace, to even be having this conversation,"* said Swamiji.

Ramlal was setting up a table in one area of the garden and announced, *"Swamiji, tea and snacks are ready, please come and eat while they're still hot. We have khichdi (lentils cooked with rice), mixed vegetable pakoras and samosas with chutney, hot gulab jamuns and hot chai,"* said Ramlal. Everyone took a break and cherished the hot snacks in the cold weather. They walked around the garden with plates in hand, occasionally looking at the beautiful full moon in a clear sky, then seeing the beautiful plants and flowers that were planted in the garden. The air was filled with mixed fragrance from the flowers.

"There can be no night better than this," thought David to himself, *"I'm in the Himalayas, at the top of a hill at 2am watching the full moon and having chai in the presence of a true Saint and discussing about God. What more could I have asked for,"* said David to himself, especially because he had never stepped out of his busy city life even for a vacation. This trip was his first time taking a break from his work, his first holiday you could say and look where he landed.

After everyone was done with the snacks, they all took their seats once again and Swamiji called out to Ramlal, *"Ramlal, one more round of only hot chai and cookies after about an hour please, we should be done by then," "Sure Swamiji,"* replied Ramlal.

Swamiji looked at everyone, *"Back to your questions of what lies on the other side of "Realizing" yourself to be Brahman. Basically you are asking what is the difference between you and an enlightened person, Sage or Saint. Would that be correct Uchit?"* asked Swamiji smiling at Uchit *"Yes Swamiji,"* replied Uchit confidently. *"David, firstly to put at rest your idea that life would be boring and dull after Self-realization, one needs to simply observe the lives of truly enlightened people."*

"One of the common characteristics is that they are always happy, smiling and in a certain kind of unexplainable bliss. They seem to be happy in all circumstances even when there doesn't seem to be any reason for happiness. Apart from that, they emit this happiness unknowingly to everyone who comes near them. You will always feel calm and loved in the company of a true saint. And still observing their lives further, you will find that they are very active in their personal lives too."

"They hardly or almost never do anything for themselves, but they cannot help but do everything in their capacity to help others, serve others, feed others, impart their knowledge and wisdom to others and try to lift them out of their misery. And this is something they cannot resist doing. So to answer your question, life doesn't become boring and dull, in fact you actually start feeling alive for the first time. You realize you are not just alive in a body but you are LIFE itself." Swamiji spoke with such compassion.

"There's a saying in all ashrams that reads 'A Sad Saint Is A Bad Saint' and I'm sure you will testify that any person you consider to be enlightened would be one of the most happiest person in the world and not because they are the wealthiest but because it is inherent of their nature. A flame can't help but be hot, a true Saint can't help but be happy. In fact money, worldly success, name and fame don't guarantee happiness. There are hundreds of famous and rich people in the world who we could call successful. They have everything that we think would make a person happy and yet many of them go into depression while a few others even commit suicide."

"There is only one kind of people who are always happy in all circumstances, without worldly objects and things, with just the bare minimum required to stay alive and that kind of people are only the Saints, Sages and Self realized or God realized people. Has anyone ever heard of a Saint going into depression or committing suicide? Couldn't have been much of a Saint if he did," laughed Swamiji and everyone burst out too.

Swamiji continued, *"I'll let you in on what more is on the other side. Remember it is not really the other side, it's the difference between the real and what "appears" to be real."*

(Taittiriya Upanishad, Part 2: Bliss of Brahman. Chapter 1 Verse 3 **"Om. He who knows Brahman attains the Highest.***)*

"The Taittiriya Upanishad (as quoted above) says, **"The Knower of Brahman attains the highest."** *This means that the one who knows Brahman achieves the highest possible achievement in the Universe, and what would that be?"*

"Let me tell you a short story; once a man meditated on God for many years, finally God did appear before him and granted him a wish in which he could ask for only one thing, what do you think he asked for? Most people would ask for worldly things like wealth, money, bigger homes, bigger cars, a world tour and so on, but he was a smart person. He asked for 'happiness in its full capacity'. God said, "Done! From now on till the end of your life you will be utmost happy always." As soon as the man heard that he realized that he had at the most another 20-30yrs more to live and he spoke to God again."

"God, I want the happiness you have granted but to enjoy it I also want it to last forever, If I die then I won't be able to enjoy it. I want to live forever in this happiness." God said, *"Done! From now on you will be utmost happy and also become immortal but you won't experience it,"* replied God, *"What? No God, I want to be utmost happy, live forever and of course experience it all,"* replied the man. *"My son, what you are asking for, you already are! Find out what you are in truth,"* came God's reply."

"The knower of Brahman realizes that he is bliss itself, that he is immortal – was never born and can never die, that he is omnipresent – all pervading, that he is omniscient – all knowing. He realizes that he is the entire Universe, that he is the underlying reality of everything in the Universe, that he himself projects the entire Universe upon himself and watches or witnesses the play of consciousness in the Universe without ever being touched or affected by what's going on. Is that possible to comprehend or even imagine from the unenlightened state? No it is not!" said Swamiji and continued.

"Furthermore, the knower of Brahman transcends all pain and suffering associated with the mind and body, he realizes his timeless nature and has no fear of death, he realizes his oneness with everything and everyone in the Universe and thus becomes fearless of anything (one cannot fear himself), he realizes that all his desires that he ever had, has and could have in the future have all been fulfilled in that one moment of realization, he has no personal desire left for anything, he realizes that whatever one could possibly want to achieve in human life he has achieved and whatever one could possibly want to know in the Universe he has known. All this is not a gradual process but it all takes place in that one moment of enlightenment, awakening or realization, instantly."

"You can compare this to a dream. You may live for sixty years in a dream, in which there's an entire Universe of objects and other people too but in that one moment of waking up from the dream you realize that the entire dream Universe was just a projection of your mind, the entire time that passed in the Universe was also created by your mind, everything and every person in your dream was only your mind. What can you desire to have from your dream when you know it was all just an appearance in your mind? All the happiness or pain and sorrow in the dream have not touched you in reality. Everything in the dream including your own dream body was not real; the reality is that you were lying on your bed dreaming all this. That is what happens in that

one moment of enlightenment. You wake up from the dream of life! You become the Buddha – The Awakened One!"

"Let me give you some more observable characteristics of the enlightened person. The enlightened person experiences the underlying 'Oneness' with everyone and everything in the Universe with the same intensity that the unenlightened person experiences himself as 'separate' from everything else in the Universe. The Saint sees the Oneness of the Universe while the ordinary person sees a million things all-separate from himself. The Sage sees himself in everything and everyone, the ordinary person sees everyone and everything outside of himself. The Saint sees everything as part of himself, the ordinary person sees everything apart from himself. The Saint sees everything within, the ordinary person sees everything without."

"Now, what happens when you see yourself as this person living in a little body with a mind? You feel separate from every object in the Universe. You are an individual and there are billions of other people and entities in the world and they all seem to be individuals as well. This is when fear steps in. You are fearful of 'other' individual people or things. This is when jealousy steps in, you want the object that the other individual seems to be enjoying. This is when desire steps in, if only I get this and that I will feel complete, happy and at ease. This is when competition steps in; I need to do better than the other person. I need to get ahead and win, not

lose. This is when selfishness steps in; I have to do things for myself before others, even if they need it more than me. All this happens when one sees themselves apart or separate from everyone and everything else, being limited to a small body and mind striving to survive in this huge competitive world."

"The enlightened person sees exactly the opposite. He has no fear of anything including death, no fear of difficult circumstances. He transcends pain and sorrow. That doesn't mean he will have no suffering, his body and mind may still suffer but it won't affect 'him' (him as Brahman) anymore because he has stopped identifying himself with the body-mind complex. He knows pain and pleasure exist only in the body and mind and he is unaffected by either. He doesn't get attached to either, but merely witnesses them arising and subsiding."

"He is unselfish, generous, compassionate and spends his life serving others and trying to make them transcend suffering as he himself has done. The true enlightened Guru will not really be blessing you with worldly riches and comforts but rather spiritual wisdom so you too can transcend the worldly sorrow and suffering by realizing your true Self and achieving the highest," said Swamiji sounding ever so polite, loving and firm at the same time.

"Does anyone have any questions?" asked Swamiji, *"The only question I have after hearing all this is how do I know Brahman in reality and experientially? I would like to transcend all pain and suffering and be one with the Universe and at peace with everyone and everything. Please Swamiji, that is what I would like to know and become,"* said Amelia with tears in her eyes.

"Since I got here, and after hearing about the One Supreme Being that you are calling Brahman, I have begun to see the divinity in everyone and everything. Everything here seems to be alive and dancing joyfully, the hills, the trees, the flowers, the people, the air and everything is like one divine play of consciousness and I have started to recognize that in whatever I'm seeing and perceiving. I want to become one with that divine play and consciousness Swamiji, and only you can help us do that," pleaded Amelia.

"My dear child, we'll keep that for another day as it will be a long discussion. For now if that's it let's have some chai and call it a night," replied Swamiji, *"Swamiji I have one question,"* said Otto, *"Sure, please ask," "What happens to us if we don't realize ourselves to be Brahman? What if we try but fail in finding out our true nature?"* asked Otto. *"Great question Otto,"* said Swamiji.

"What happens if you strive but don't experience that instant moment of enlightenment? What becomes your fate after this life then? Well the scriptures tell us that one will go from death to death, which means that one will be reborn again and again until they 1) are re-born as a human being again and 2) realize their true nature, merge with the Source and end this cycle of birth and rebirth."

"Every soul has to merge back into that one divine Supreme Being, some do it quicker than others. This is the purpose of the human birth that we have been given. It's the single most important thing you can do for all of humanity as well because the enlightened person does for others what no other human being can do, which is guide them back to their Source," said Swamiji.

"Any steps one may take towards God or realizing their true nature doesn't go wasted, so say the scriptures, when one is re-born in the human form again, they pick up again from where they left and work their way towards that Supreme Being", said Swamiji. *"Time for tea,"* said Ramlal, walking into the garden, *"It's quite cold and past 4am in the morning. Please have some tea to warm yourselves."*

They all got up and went towards the table that had been laid out and Ramlal served everyone with hot steaming *chai* and cookies. Swamiji finished his cup and announced, *"I will see you all on Monday now. I have to go out on the weekend for some work and will be back on Monday. Till then Ramlal will look after you in case you need anything."*

"Oh I just remembered Swamiji," said David, *"I met someone in the market named Aabha and he spoke about you too. He asked me to visit the Panshuls Fair that takes place on the weekends, would it be advisable to go there? He said it is a fun place for anyone trying to realize the Self."*

"Oh yes, Panshul is an awakened being too, he has this fun way of pointing someone to realize the Self. He always looked at life as a game and after his own realization of the Self he created a set of interesting games that will make you think about the reality from a different perspective. You should definitely visit it today or tomorrow and we'll talk about it on Monday," said Swamiji and took leave. He walked off towards his room and in a short while so did everyone else. It had been a long day and night for all of them as the lights in all the rooms went off one by one.

I AM BRAHMAN

PANSHUL'S FAIR

The whole of Saturday morning was spent sleeping, with Ramlal delivering breakfast to each room. They all gathered together for dinner in the dining hall and although Swamiji was not present, everyone ate in silence maintaining the same discipline as they had when Swamiji was present. After dinner they all met out in the lawn and as they enjoyed taking a stroll around the garden they all planned to go visit Panshul's Fair in the morning. David suggested they have their morning tea at Ramlal's secret Sunrise hilltop. He wanted to see the sun rise there as many times as he could while he was at the ashram.

All was planned and in the morning at 5:30am they all made their way out of the ashram, following Ramlal in the dim light. He led them along the road and then through the bushes towards the steep hill. Everyone gasped for breath as they climbed the last part of the hill to step at the top. Otto had to be helped up by Ramlal as he wasn't so physically fit. As they all stood facing the deep valley before them with the Sun once again beginning to pierce the sky with its first rays, everyone was awestruck. Oliver and Amelia were holding hands and seemed to be reciting a prayer. Otto sat down with his eyes and mouth wide open at the beautiful scenery set before them.

Slowly the golden light started to fill the entire horizon. Shades of Red, orange, yellow and gold spread out in the sky. Birds were chirping and singing in the trees, butterflies and dragonflies flew excitedly over the luscious green grass that was wet with morning dew. Ramlal poured out the tea in cups and handed them out to everyone.

"What a sight!" exclaimed Oliver. *"This is what I want to do with you every single day of my life!"* whispered Amelia resting her head on Oliver's chest. In the next few minutes the Sun had fully risen and the entire valley was brought to life once again. *"Sunrises are so beautiful,"* said Otto, *"The sunrise doesn't care whether we watch it or not. It keeps on being beautiful even if no one bothers to look at it,"* said Ramlal. They all sat there in silence absorbing and appreciating mother nature as they sipped the hot tea.

"It's time to go," said Ramlal and they all slowly climbed back down the steep hill and walked back to the ashram. Everyone freshened up and was ready for Panshul's Fair. The twenty-minute walk towards the market was a quick one, *"We need to get to the northern end of the market and we better hurry if you want to see the entire fair today,"* said Ramlal hastening his walk. As they walked through the streets, from a distance they could see a huge arch shaped iron gate with a sign board that read, *"Panshul's Fair – Come Find Yourself Today!"*

As they walked through the gate there were already around sixty people who had lined up at the ticket counter to buy tickets to go inside. From the outside it looked like a large ground floor building that probably had many smaller rooms inside for the games and entertainment. People seemed excited outside, talking away happily and children played with each other. There were more foreigners than local Indians in the queue. *"It's quite expensive for the local Indians to afford the entry fee, so you'll find mostly tourists lined up to go in. It's mainly a tourist attraction and one of its kind in the country,"* said Ramlal as they all stood in line for their turn.

Ramlal collected the three hundred rupees per person from everyone and purchased the tickets and they walked in through a black iron door that had a man dressed up in a three-piece black suit and tie with a matching hat. He resembled an English gentleman from the colonial times. Wearing white gloves he took the tickets and welcomed everyone into the fair with the saying, *"Welcome To Panshul's Fair, be warned, once inside we don't guarantee you'll come out the same,"* he said as he bowed down and waved his hand towards the door.

They all walked in and it seemed like they had all entered a maze with pitch dark walls leading to numerous rooms that had a little sign board at the top saying what room it was.

The first room they entered was called the *"Horror Hall"* in which only five people were allowed in at a time. As they were all together in a queue, all five of them managed to get into the room as one group. A man pointed to a board with three rules of the game and announced that they had ten minutes to complete the task.

The rules were:
1. Find the headless body as soon as you can.
2. Rush to the Exit door once you find it.
3. The first to do so will win a special hamper.

A siren was sounded and the man opened a door that led into a large hall that had dummies all over the place, almost over two hundred full sized dummies that were fully clothed were all over the floor. Many piled up on top of each other. Everyone dashed in and started their search for the headless body. Uchit was quite fast as he started from one corner working his way across the hall, checking each dummy before throwing it back. Oliver and Amelia worked as a team and later Otto and Uchit worked together for a while but David stood in the center of the hall looking around with precision vision trying to scan all the dummies for the headless one.

At the end of ten minutes another siren sounded and they were directed towards the exit door by the same man. None of them had managed to find it. Oliver and Amelia didn't manage to go through all the dummies, Uchit swore he had gone through all the dummies and the whole game was a fraud. Otto hadn't seen them all while David too thought he did manage to see most of the dummies but none without a head.

They were soon directed to the next room through a dark corridor. The second door had a signboard that read, *"The Process of Creation"*. As they walked in they read the rules board.
The rules were:
1. Use the clay provided to create different things.
2. Place what you create in the tray provided.
3. Write the number of new things you created.
4. Winner will be announced at the end of the fair.

I AM BRAHMAN

They had twenty minutes to create as many things they could out of a huge lump of clay they were each provided with. The siren sounded and they all started with their creative skills, it reminded them all of their childhood when they played with play-dough. It was fun doing it again after so many years. Uchit made the most things in twenty minutes that included a pot, an elephant, a cup and saucer, a basket, a little boy, a small hut, a boat and a car.

At the end when the siren went off, Uchit had made eighteen things, Amelia managed twelve, Oliver made ten, Otto managed six and David created only five. They each placed their items and wrote how many new things they had created from the clay with their names on the tray. Uchit seemed like a clear winner for this one.

This was getting interesting and fun too. The next room had a signboard at the top, which read, *"Pray & Meet God Here"*. Only one person was allowed in at a time.

The rules were:
1. Leave your "EGO" here and step in.
2. Pray to God and He WILL appear in the mirror.
3. When the light turns red, exit the room.
4. Describe the God you saw.
5. Submit your description and go to the next room.

Oliver was the first to go in. This was a small room with only one sofa chair. The room was sound proof and a green light indicated that the person can stay inside and had to exit when it turned red. Oliver entered and sat on the sofa, he looked at his reflection in the mirror opposite the chair. He then went on his knees, folded his hands and prayed but kept his eyes open. He prayed and prayed but no one appeared. All he could see was his own reflection in the mirror. Three minutes were up and the light turned red. Oliver exited the room disappointed; he wrote down the following, *"No God appeared even after I prayed sincerely with all my heart. I only saw myself in the mirror. I saw nothing else. This was a dumb game."*

Next to go in was Amelia, she went on her knees and prayed with her eyes closed but occasionally looking at the mirror to see if anyone appeared. Soon time was up and the note she submitted read, *"Maybe I was not sincere enough for God to appear."*

Next in was Otto and at the end of his time his note read, *"I don't think God appears like this, stop making fools of the innocent public."* In went Uchit and stood before the mirror, he decided not to sit on the sofa, instead he kept staring in the mirror to see if it was a one sided mirror. He thought someone at the back of the mirror would appear claiming to be God. He looked and looked from top to bottom but couldn't find anything. His time was up too and he went out in a fury without writing anything.

I AM BRAHMAN

David went in next and sat on the sofa. He tried praying but it didn't sound believable to him that God would appear in the mirror before him. He half-heartedly prayed for some time, looked in the mirror to see if anything appeared but there was only a reflection of himself. The light turned red and he too stepped out and wrote down, *"I didn't see God as promised. There was only a reflection of me and no one else in the mirror for the entire the time."*

They all walked along another dark corridor towards a door with the signboard that read, *"Picture Stories"*. They all walked in and a man handed each of them a drawing paper, some color pencils, paint and paintbrushes. They could spend up to forty minutes for this task.

The rules were:
1. Draw or paint something that tells a story.
2. Note down the truth about your drawing.
3. Submit your drawing/painting and note.
4. Winner will be revealed at the end of the fair.

Everyone set out to make their drawing and painting as spectacular as possible. David painted a lovely picture of a man in hospital who was hugging his wife after a successful heart surgery. His note at the end was, *"The truth is that no one can guarantee life."*

Amelia painted a lovely bedroom with a window from which one could see the moon and a few stars. There was a little fairy with a magic wand spraying magic dust into the bedroom. It reminded her of her childhood when she knew that fairies visited and spoke to her in her bedroom at bedtime but they no longer appeared after a few years and she missed them. Her note at the end read, *"The truth is that angels and fairies look after little children till they are capable of looking after themselves."*

Otto wasn't good at drawing but he managed to draw a car and a truck in an accident, a man behind the wheel and a woman lying in a pool of blood outside the car, it was a gruesome sight. This was how his wife had passed away and he remembered the scene very well. A speeding truck had hit them and she died on the spot. His note at the end was, *"The truth is that you can suffer because of someone else's mistake."*

Uchit painted a landscape with a few hills, dark clouds and rain. He also painted several rivers flowing down the hills into the ocean. His note at the end was, *"The truth is that every river flows into the ocean and becomes the ocean."* Oliver painted a beautiful Australian seaside with a few couples on the beach and two little children playing in the sand. He still had a memory of when he had first met Amelia when their parents took them to the seaside. His note at the end was, *"The truth is that true love can happen at any age."* After a good forty minutes spent perfecting their drawings and paintings, they handed in their artwork and notes, leaving through the exit door.

The next corridor led them into a canteen that was selling snacks and beverages. It was lunchtime and they were all hungry. Apart from that they had just been through half of the fair and it was a good time to eat something before going any further. Oliver and Amelia grabbed some sandwiches; Otto bought a vanilla cup cake with coffee. David and Uchit settled for some local rice pudding called *'dalia'*. They all discussed what had happened so far and none could make out exactly what was the purpose of the tasks given. Aabha had told David that it would be a fun way to realize the Self, Swamiji had said the same but nothing so far was even close to helping one realize the Self, in fact it all felt fun but childish and silly.

They decided to go through it all anyway and give it their best shot. After their short break, they headed for the next door along the corridor, the signboard above this door read, *"Tat Tvam Asi – That Thou Art"*. The door opened to a living room set up with sofa chairs, a floor rug under the coffee table, pictures on the wall, a television, a flower vase with a variety of fresh flowers and a standing lamp on the side.
The rules were:
1. Identify everything that is 'that'.
2. Replace everything that is 'that' with 'you'.
3. Write down how many things there are in total.

They all walked in together and looked around. They had ten minutes to scan and find the answer. After two minutes they gathered around the coffee table and discussed what the rules actually meant. *"Everything we can see is 'that',"* said Oliver, *"That table, that television, that chair, that vase, that wall, that lamp. Everything here can be classified as 'that',"* said Oliver. *"Next it says, replace everything that is 'that' with 'you'. So that means everything I see here is me. I am everything and everything is I. So the answer to how many things are here should be one! This task is talking about Brahman. Swamiji already explained Tat Tvam Asi to us. This task must be to help us identify oneness with everything and our true Brahman nature,"* said Oliver. Everyone agreed as they had just had this lesson with Swamiji a day earlier. Well, it was the first task they understood clearly.

They all proceeded to the next door where the signboard read, *"Who Are You?"* They were all handed sheets of paper and a pen each as they entered the room; there were desks like in a classroom. After all the desks were occupied, a man walked in and wrote the rules on the blackboard in front of them.
The rules were:
1. Write five sentences about yourself each beginning with the words 'I am....'
2. Write down a conclusion of who you actually are in just five words."

I AM BRAHMAN

Everyone wrote down different things about themselves and their conclusions were quite amusing. Otto concluded, *"I am a widower."* Oliver concluded, *"I am a lover."* Amelia concluded, *"I am Australian."* Uchit concluded, *"I am a fighter,"* and David who had understood the game concluded, *"I am..."*

They all handed their papers and walked out into the dark corridor again that led to the last door. It had a sign saying *"Enjoy The Movie"*. Twenty five people were allowed in at one time into the mini theatre which was surprisingly equipped with a top notch large screen and a great sound system. They all took their seats and the show begun. An Indian man in his late fifties with a baldhead, wearing a grey suit walked onto the screen. With a typical British accent he introduced himself.

PANSHUL'S TALK

"Hi everyone, my name is Panshul and I hope you had a great time here today. You might have found some of the tasks asked of you today a little childish, boring or even stupid. You were asked to answer some questions that no one has ever asked you before, but believe me, these very questions are the answers to all your problems in life. They are the questions that not even our parents, teachers, employers, colleagues and friends ask themselves or us. We take a lot of what life offers us for granted, not paying the least attention to what really is in front of us or appreciating the experiences we go through daily," said Panshul.

"I won't take much of your time but would like to walk with you through all the rooms and the tasks that you have performed and let's see if we can see more than just what meets the eye. In the Horror Hall you were asked to find the

headless body in the hall. I'm sure you must've struggled through all the dummies, but in ten minutes you couldn't have gone through all of them. There are over five hundred dummies in that hall and ten minutes is too less to even glance at each one. If you were clever and alert, upon entering you would have immediately identified yourself as being the headless body. In this mini theatre hall right now, look around and spot the headless body. You can see everyone's head but your own. Often when someone asks us who we are or we take the time to figure out who we are, we always look outside to see who or what we are. The only person in the world you can never see is YOU because you can only BE you."

"After that you went into the "Process of Creation" room. This must have taken you back to your childhood days when you played with clay and made your favorite toys. It's a very relaxing activity. I'm sure you must've made lovely items out of the clay. Items that you made when you were young and other items that you like now. The question asked at the end of the task was, "How many new things did you create?" And many of you would have created five, ten or even twenty different objects, which is impressive, but the real answer is ZERO! No matter what you did with the clay, whatever you put in the tray at the end was nothing but clay. Let's take a closer look at what new things you think you might have created."

The background scene had changed and Panshul was now standing in the 'Process of Creation' room with a lineup of items created with clay on a tabletop in front of him. He picked up a beautiful pot, *"This is awesome creativity, an actual clay pot. Let's examine what 'new thing' was 'created' by the person who made this. The sides are all clay, the belly is round and made of clay, the bottom is clay, the inside and outside is all nothing but clay. In fact the entire pot is nothing else but clay. A lump of clay was transformed into some 'thing' called a pot. But really, was a new 'thing' created?"*

"A thing is one that can be shown separately from another thing, for example, I can show you this table and this pot, they can be separated from one another and hence they are two separate things. The table is one thing and the pot is another. But that doesn't apply to the pot and clay. We cannot separate the clay from the pot. The pot is nothing but clay. If you take the clay out of the pot, there is no pot that remains. 'Pot' is a 'name' given to this 'form' of clay that has a particular use. The pot is not a new 'thing' that was created; it is nothing but clay in this form. In fact now if you see, all the items here are nothing but clay. In all these items made of clay here, the "reality" of all of them is clay. Thus there is NO new 'thing' CREATED, everything on this table is nothing but clay," said Panshul.

"After that you headed to the "Pray & Meet God Here" room, where you were asked to leave your "ego" outside before stepping in. How many of you actually left your ego outside? Maybe some did and some of you didn't, but when you entered the room, everyone must've seen their own body's reflection in the mirror. If you thought during the exercise or after stepping outside that all you saw was a reflection of YOU, then you carried your ego with you inside. If you did leave your ego even for a moment, you would have seen God looking back at you. God or Brahman looks exactly like you WITHOUT YOUR EGO. Take the ego out of you and in truth all that will be left is the divine Supreme Being. You are divinity itself, but your ego thinks otherwise."

"Try this simple exercise when you return home. Think of all the things that you think about yourself, then one by one, mentally delete them and check if YOU are still there. For example, your ego might tell you, I am an engineer, I am a lovable, kindhearted person, I have a wife and two kids, I live in Europe. I am intelligent and so on. Mentally erase all of them one by one and see what's left at the end. If I were not an engineer, would I still exist? If I were neither lovable nor kind, would I still exist? If I were neither a husband nor a father, would I still exist? If I didn't live in Europe, would I still exist? If I were not intelligent, would I still exist? Find out 'who' or 'what' still exists after taking out everything you know or think about yourself (your ego). God or Brahman looks like YOU without your ego!"

Everyone was stunned by the answers Panshul was revealing on the screen. The background changed to the Picture Stories Room and Panshul continued, *"I have seen some incredible drawings, sketches and paintings being made in this room over the past few years and I hope you too, had fun expressing yourself through pictures. Usually people draw or paint a picture of something that is close to their heart, something they might have experienced, desired or even imagined and every picture tells a story. It will invoke an emotion in the seer's mind and the mind will either feel happy, sad, disturbed, hurt, intrigued, inspired, motivated or any other emotion as a reaction to the picture."*

"You were also asked to "Note down the 'truth' about your drawing." Just to let you know, no one till date has ever answered this correctly, so if you're answer is also not what I am about to reveal don't be upset because we are just not conditioned to think this way. There is only one right answer about the truth of all your drawings. The truth about each and every drawing and painting is the DRAWING PAPER! Some of you may be surprised, let me explain quickly. Your painting is possible only because of the drawing paper. What you painted is the expression of some thoughts in your mind. What you feel when you look at the painting is the emotion connected with that particular picture. Everything on the paper is an imagination and expression, the only 'real thing' in my hand is PAPER," said Panshul holding up a lovely sunrise painting.

"In the same way pure consciousness is the drawing paper on which the body and mind paint your life. Without the drawing paper there is no painting, without consciousness there is no you! You are pure consciousness with a body and mind, just like this is a drawing paper with pictures and paint on it. The pictures and the colors are not the reality like paper, in the same way the body and mind are not the reality like consciousness."

"This is the next room that you came into," said Panshul and the background changed to the *"Tat Tvam Asi"* room, *"where many different things that you see almost daily are placed and you were asked to identify everything that you can refer to as 'that'. Then you were to replace everything that you labeled as 'that' with 'you'. The Vedantic saying 'Tat Tvam Asi' means 'That Thou Art' or 'That You Are' or 'You Are That'. They all mean the same thing. Many Saints and Gurus interpret this in complex ways but I wanted this to be very simple and therefore this was an easy task and the right answer you should have arrived to is, One thing remains which is YOU. Every other thing in the room apart from you can be labeled as 'that' and everything that is 'that', is you, so everything eventually is YOU. The only way that is possible in life is if you understand what Brahman is and realize yourself as Brahman. Once you realize Brahman, you will know everything to be you or you to be everything."*

"The next task was also an easy one where you had to write down five sentences about yourself starting with 'I am' and then condense and summarize them in less than five words. I am a man, I am a woman, I am abc and xyz. The ultimate undeniable reality is that you ARE. What you are can be argued upon but the fact that you ARE cannot be denied. Therefore the undeniable reality of any sentence you wrote down should be, "I am.."

"The last room in the fair is the one you are sitting in right now. It's a mini theatre with a screen at the front and a projector projecting the pictures you can see on the screen. Pay attention to the screen now, on my right hand side a burning flame has appeared, we'll let it burn here for some time, on my left hand side a waterfall has appeared, behind me the sun has started to shine brightly. I will now disappear and a heartwarming scene will appear here in the center of the screen, watch it and I'll be back."

Panshul disappeared as a newborn baby appeared on the screen, it was being held upside down and a doctor was seen slapping it a few times. It didn't cry and everyone in the hospital room looked worried. The doctor had given up hope and finally placed the lifeless baby in the mother's arms. As she held him with tears in her eyes, she gently placed it on her chest and the baby kicked, she held it tighter and the baby kicked a couple more times before it burst out crying, everyone was filled with joy and the doctor too was astonished at the baby coming to life. Everyone in the mini theatre clapped and some were already in tears.

On the screen using time-lapse, the baby grew into a beautiful young woman, met a man and they romanced and she was pregnant with a baby, they both looked so good and happy together. In the next scene the man was seen helping his wife cross the road, holding her hand, going towards the hospital and suddenly BANG!

A bus that jumped the traffic lights hit them and they both lay dead on the road in a pool of blood. With the sound effects in the mini theatre everyone seated was shocked too. Panshul appeared immediately on the screen with a smile, *"Relax, it was just a scene from a popular movie."*

"Let's relate this experience to real life. We go through many ups and downs in life, joy and sorrow. The body and mind experience them all without affecting YOU in any way. You may not agree with that and I'll use this mini theatre as an example. All the pictures in the movie are projected on to the screen. Joys and sorrows take place by watching what's projected on the screen, it could be anything from volcano eruptions, alien invasions, earthquakes, romance, love, evil deeds and anything you can imagine can be projected on the screen."

"Everything goes on on the screen without ever affecting the screen at all. This fire on my right hasn't burnt any part of the screen and neither has the waterfall on my left wet any part of the screen. The movie scene made you smile, happy, joyful and also made you sad and shocked, yet the screen remained undisturbed. The screen is like consciousness on which the movie of your life is playing. If you identify yourself with the body and mind then you will continue to suffer along with the body and mind. If you identify yourself as your true nature, consciousness, then the movie of your life won't affect you in any way ever. Realize yourself as pure consciousness and be free from the pain and sorrow of the body and mind. Set yourself free of the false person that you think you are!"

The movie ended and the lights came on. Panshul walked and the entire audience stood and applauded him. Another man walked in behind him with a bunch of balloons in his hand. He handed out a blown up balloon and a pin to each person in the mini theatre. After handing out around twenty-five balloons and pins he walked out smiling. Panshul addressed everyone,

"Thank you for coming to the fair. I hope you enjoyed the games; they all have hidden meanings, which if understood properly, will change your life for the best. If you realize yourself as you truly are, which is consciousness, you will transcend all pain and suffering and enjoy your life like you enjoy a movie, untouched and unaffected by what happens on the screen." said

Panshul.

"Let me explain them one by one. The headless man's message is that, not everything is an object of perception, sometimes it's the subject you're looking for, learn to look inwards too."

"The message of the clay creation is that a name and form of an object isn't the reality of that object, investigate and you'll find the name and form have no reality to it. For example, this chair is nothing but wood in reality, there is no 'thing' called a chair which is apart from the wood."

"In the EGO room, the message is very clear but few people will understand it. Your ego is preventing you from seeing God or Brahman as He, She or It should be seen. In your mind and body, either your ego can dwell or God, there's no space for both."

"In the Picture painting task, the message is that no matter what picture your life paints for you, you are the unaffected consciousness like the drawing paper on which everything is painted but it remains unaffected by what is painted on it. A painting of the ocean will not wet the paper nor will a painting of the sun burn the paper."

"Tat Tvam Asi, when you realize yourself to be Brahman, there will be nothing that you will see apart from you, it's good to know this reality before you realize it so that when the realization comes, the transition is much easier and not shocking."

"In the I am... sentences game, the message is that before you can even say your name, you have to acknowledge your existence, hence you can say I am John or Peter. The 'I am' cannot change which means that you may doubt the existence of everything in the Universe, you can even doubt the existence of God or Brahman, but you can never doubt your own existence. Find out who or what the 'I am...' refers to. (I = consciousness, am = existence)."

"In this mini theatre the message is similar to the drawing paper game. Your true nature, consciousness, is ever unchanging and untouched by whatever movie is playing on the screen. Realize your true nature as pure consciousness and enjoy the movie of your life."

"Now, before you leave, we still have to announce the winner of the hamper as promised." Panshul picked up a basket with some goodies in it and said, *"You all have a balloon and a pin in your hands. A hamper like this will be given to the person who still has his or her balloon intact at the end of five minutes. When I blow the whistle your time will start and at the end of five minutes whoever has a balloon still filled with air can collect their hamper at the exit."* He blew the whistle and everyone jumped out of their seats and started popping each other's balloons. A fun struggle went on for almost three minutes and by the fourth minute all the balloons had been popped.

Everyone sat back on their seats disappointed but Panshul had a smile on his face, *"It's a pity that no one won, but I hope you will remember a simple life lesson from this activity. Had all of you simply sat in your seats and waited for five minutes to get over, EVERYONE would have won a hamper. But instead you all thought of the opposite and popped each other's balloons simply because you had a pin in your hand. We are always looking to get ahead of others in life even if it means pulling them down to get ahead. We can all be happy together if we focus on ourselves rather than others. This balloon game will remind you that to win you don't need to necessarily defeat someone else."*

"Everyone can focus on their own life and as a result everybody could be a winner in the game of life. Apply that in your life and you'll find more joyful people around you. Thank you very much and have a great evening, and as a token of appreciation and souvenir from Panshul's Fair, everyone will still get a hamper." Everyone clapped and whistled in joy as Panshul walked towards the exit door. He gave each person a warm hug and a hamper as everyone exited one by one with a smile on their face. It was a day well spent and like Ramlal said, *"It was truly one of its kind in the country."*

Back at the ashram it was dinner time and everyone sat in the dining hall as usual and had the simple *dal chawal* that had been prepared, followed by a bowl of *'kheer'*, a sweet milk based dessert. After dinner everyone washed their used utensils at the wash basin before heading out towards the garden for a stroll. Ramlal came into the garden and quickly stacked up some firewood and lit up a large bonfire. Everyone sat around it at the top of the hill in the Himalayas as a lovely romantic ambience was created.

Otto dashed towards his room and was soon back with a guitar in his hand. He played and sung some old European love ballads as some couples clapped, others danced around the fire while Oliver and Amelia sat on the grass holding hands staring at the sky filled with millions of stars. Everyone was absorbed in the beautiful mystic ambience. Swamiji would be back the next day to discuss with them the most important part so far, which was how to realize Brahman and attain spiritual enlightenment. But for now, singing, talking and laughter was heard from the ashram garden and around the Himalayan hilltop as they danced and made merry till the wee hours of the morning.

I AM BRAHMAN

EXTRA NOTES

This is the end of part two of the series, "I Am Consciousness." This part contains many gems (nuggets of the Absolute Reality) that can lead to Self- Realization and God-Realization. The realization that there is only One Absolute Reality in the Universe and that reality is YOUR own reality. It is One Pure Consciousness that is projecting the entire Universe upon itself and witnessing it without being affected at all, just like the screen is ever unaffected by the movie playing on it.

This is a remarkable claim and with all the facts presented one cannot deny it in any manner. It is the same realization that all the Saints and Sages have given us in the past expressing them in different words.

If you understood most of what was said in this part then, sayings such as, "the whole world is an illusion," will become very clear and easy to understand. By the end of this little book, (assuming you read the 1st part as well), you, the reader should be clear as to what Brahman – the Absolute Reality is, how to recognize this Supreme Being everywhere, every time and in everything. You should have understood now that the same Brahman is YOUR true identity. You should have intellectually and philosophically grasped this (read the parts you don't understand a second time and a third time till it makes sense logically and you can't refute what's being said.)

Having said that, you need NOT be experiencing what's been said directly at this point, if you are, a huge thumbs up to you. Because if just intellectual knowledge was sufficient for spiritual enlightenment all the scholars who are learned in depth would be enlightened but they're not. Philosophical knowledge alone will not set you free or give you liberation, salvation, nirvana or enlightenment.

It's not impossible but the mind would have to be in a very, very pure state, for only knowledge to enlighten someone, and that would be a very rare case. There are many preparations or ground work that need to be done by the majority of us before this acquired knowledge becomes a living reality for us.

In the 3rd installment of this series titled, "Prepare To Awaken", Swamiji will talk about what is standing between you and God that will not allow the union to take place. David learns many different ways that help purify the mind and prepare it for that one moment when God's grace breaks through and an incredible union takes place. This is Yoga. Yoga refers to 'union' with the Absolute. We look forward to you joining David on this fascinating spiritual journey that puts all the great wisdom of the Upanishads in a smooth flowing story format for easier understanding.

ABOUT THE AUTHOR

Sukhdev Virdee was born and brought up in Nairobi, Kenya. Since childhood he was very inclined towards spirituality and music. After his studies he chose to take up music as a profession. He learnt how to play the keyboards and started performing live on stage at the age of nineteen. He later went to London and completed a BTEC in Music Production and Performance.

He later flew to Mumbai, India to pursue his dream of singing and composing music in the largest Indian Entertainment Industry. His debut pop-album became a chartbuster making him a popular household name in India and across the world. Mumbai became his home where he is known for his high energy live performances and this popularity took him to several countries across every continent on the planet to perform live for huge audiences.

A few more albums and singles followed after that. He was living the life that every young person looks up to even today. He had created a name for himself and enjoyed the name, fame and fortune that most singers dream of but never get to live. During all this he was totally oblivious of what life had in store for him in the coming years.

Just before his 40th birthday, when he was going through a rather rough patch in life, three of his friends gifted him the Bhagavad Gita out of the blue. These were friends that he met only occasionally and yet within two weeks three different people gifted him the Bhagavad Gita which would change his life completely. He read the Bhagavad Gita and felt Lord Krishna was speaking directly to him. It completely changed his outlook towards life as he followed the teachings in the Bhagavad Gita as best as he could.

Just over a year later, one fine morning after he woke up from his morning meditation and walked towards his temple in the house, his body completely froze and in an instant he had become one with the entire Universe. Time stood still and every particle of the entire Universe was alive and shining in bright golden light and he was the light. He was no longer limited to just his body or mind, he was everywhere at the same time and everything was one with him.

This Spiritual awakening experience turned his life upside down and inside out. All desires for anything worldly vanished, fear of death vanished, love and compassion for entire humanity and nature arose and he could feel and experience the Supreme Being in everything.

Not knowing exactly what had happened and what to do next, he sought out several resources before he was pointed towards the Upanishads which answered all his questions as to what had happened, what led to it and what to do after such an awakening.

After years of studying the Vedanta texts he is now an expert on non-dual Vedanta through not only intellectual and philosophical knowledge but most importantly with his own personal direct experience every day.

He has put all his heart and soul into writing the *"I Am Consciousness"* book series that include the highest knowledge of the Upanishads and his own direct experience and knowledge of the Supreme Being.

The series has been written with the absolute conviction that you, the reader, can realize your true immortal Universal Self too, that you are pure bliss and completely unaffected by all pain and suffering.

The promise of all spirituality is that one transcends pain and sorrow in this world, not that pain and sorrow don't come, but that the realized being is untouched by it. One realizes that their true nature is immortal, that they are one with the Universe. Would a being who realizes that he or she is one with the Universe ever want to accumulate anything in this world?

No, the True Saint or Sage who is Self-Realized makes do with only the very basic necessities required to live an honest decent life. They don't look to gain wealth, become famous, build an empire or any such sort of selfish activities.

Their main focus becomes serving humanity selflessly and uplifting others to help them realize their true nature so that they too can transcend suffering and realize their Oneness with the Universe. Sukhdev aims to do just that through his music, art and writing in the remaining days that he has left in this mortal body.

"I Am Consciousness"
6 Book Series
A Journey From Seeker
To Enlightened Master
Available As
E-books & Paperbacks
On Amazon & Other Digital Stores

Available As
E-books & Paperbacks
On Amazon & Other Digital Stores

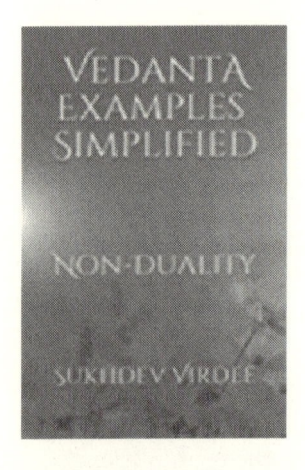

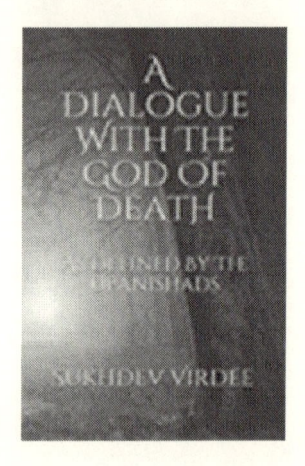

VEDANTA EXAMPLES SIMPLIFIED

NON-DUALITY

SUKHDEV VIRDEE

THE DAY I MET GURU NANAK

NON-DUALITY

SUKHDEV VIRDEE

THE POWER OF NOTHING

NON-DUALITY

SUKHDEV VIRDEE

A DIALOGUE WITH THE GOD OF DEATH

AS DEFINED BY THE UPANISHADS

SUKHDEV VIRDEE

Made in the USA
Middletown, DE
11 November 2024